# Motive power recognition: 3

# DMUs

## Colin J. Marsden

Front cover:
*Class 142 two-car multiple-unit No 142.001 photographed at Loughborough station on 17 May 1985. This was the day on which the unit was handed over at Derby Litchurch Lane works.* C. J. Tuffs

Back cover, top:
*Class 121 DMBS No 55020 was repainted in chocolate & cream livery for the GWR 150 celebrations in 1985. It is seen at Reading.* Colin J. Marsden

Back cover, bottom:
*Production Class 150 unit No 150.102 on a crew training run at Kettering on 21 October 1985.* Adrian Vaughan

First published 1982

This Edition 1986

ISBN 0 7110 1570 8

All rights reserved. No part of this book may be reproduced or transmitted in any form or by any means, electronic or mechanical, including photocopying, recording or by any information storage and retrieval system, without permission from the Publisher in writing.

© Ian Allan Ltd 1986

Published by Ian Allan Ltd, Shepperton, Surrey; and printed by Ian Allan Printing Ltd at their works at Coombelands in Runnymede, England

Right:
*The most numerous DMMU type in service is the Metro-Cammell Class 101, allocated to all regions except the SR. Front end detail:*
***1** Front marker lights (also able to show red to act as tail indicators), **2** Vacuum reservoir pipe, **3** Vacuum train pipe, **4** Electrical control jumper cable (in dummy), **5** As No 4, **6** Screw coupling, **7** Electrical control jumper socket, **8** As No 7, **9** Air warning horn, **10** Control air pipe.* Colin J. Marsden

Far right:
*Presently being used on the WR are the two Class 210 prototype diesel-electric sets built by BR and introduced in 1981. These sets incorporate an above-floor engine at one end of each set. All coaches are fitted with air-operated sliding doors. The 3-coach set No 210.002 stands at Paddington on 1 November 1984 with the 16.03 local service to Reading.*
Colin J. Marsden

# Introduction

The recognition and identification of the various types, coaches and formations of the BR Diesel Multiple-Unit fleet is probably the most difficult of all motive power types. The majority of cars are of the same basic layout, except for a handful of cross-country sets, and the average traveller and indeed many enthusiasts, do not know whether they are travelling in, or looking at, a low or high density vehicle, or if it was built by BR, Metro-Cammell, Birmingham RC&W or Cravens, etc. This second edition of the third volume in the *Motive Power Recognition* series sets out to try and give readers some basic assistance in recognising these different types/classes.

DMUs are divided into two distinct groups: those fitted with an underfloor engine and a mechanical transmission (DMMU), and those fitted with an engine-room mounted prime mover where the diesel engine drives a generator which in turn produces electrical power for underslung traction motors (DEMU).

Numbering of mechanical vehicles is achieved by individual coach numbers. Most WR and ScR DMMU vehicles run in numbered sets but these cannot be relied upon for accuracy when trying to identify individual cars, as misformations are frequently reported. The latest built Classes 150 and 151 sets also carry set numbers and it is expected that subsequent production fleets of 'new generation' units will follow suit. All DEMU 'sets' carry unit numbers on their ends.

In early 1985 over 2,700 cars of DMU stock were in traffic. Whilst in recent years this figure has dropped following heavy withdrawals, the figure is envisaged to remain fairly constant over the coming years, with considerable investment in new types being committed.

This book has been prepared with the view that all sets are running with their correct type coaches, but this is unlikely to happen in day-to-day operation, and over the years on more than one occasion the Author has recorded a 3-car set in traffic formed of vehicles from three different classes.

I would like to take this opportunity to thank the many people who have assisted in the research and preparation of material for this book. My special thanks go to Michael Collins and John Tuffs who, with my list of requirements in hand, have gone out specially to take photographs of specific vehicles. It is hoped that readers of this volume will find it useful in the observation and recognition of the diesel unit classes and thus make their interest in railways more enjoyable.

The Editor of this volume would like to be notified of any major detail differences that have been omitted, by sending them together with a photograph if possible, to the Editor, c/o Ian Allan Ltd, Coombelands House, Addlestone, Weybridge, Surrey KT15 1HY.

**Colin J. Marsden**
Worcester Park
October 1985

# Diesel Multiple-Unit Coach Classifications

| | |
|---|---|
| DHBS | Driving Half (motor) brake second |
| DHC | Driving Half (motor) composite |
| DM | Driving motor |
| DMB | Driving motor brake |
| DMBC | Driving motor brake composite |
| DMBF | Driving motor brake first |
| DMBS | Driving motor brake second |
| DMC | Driving motor composite |
| DMLV | Driving motor luggage van |
| DMS | Driving motor second |
| DTC | Driving trailer composite |
| DTS | Driving trailer second |
| MBS | Motor brake second |
| MS | Motor second |
| TBS | Trailer brake second |
| TC | Trailer composite |
| TF | Trailer first |
| TGS | Trailer guards second |
| TFLK | Trailer first lounge kitchen |
| TRSB | Trailer second buffet |
| TRUB | Trailer unclassified buffet |
| TRUK | Trailer unclassified kitchen |
| TS | Trailer second |

**Train type codes**

| | |
|---|---|
| CC | Cross Country |
| HD | High Density |
| HST | High Speed Train |
| LD | Low Density |
| PCLS | Parcels |

Above:
*Pressed Steel built, WR allocated, Class 117 3-car set No L415 with its DMBS leading, passes Acton West on 12 August 1984 with a Reading-Paddington train.*
Colin J. Marsden

# Diesel Multiple-Unit Types and Vehicles

| *Class* | *Type* | *Car Types* | *Regions of Allocation* |
|---|---|---|---|
| 100 | LD | DMBS | Midland |
| 101 | LD | DMBS, DMC, DTC, TBS, TC, TS | Midland/Eastern/Western/Scottish |
| 104 | LD | DMBS, DMC, DTC, TBS, TC, TS, DHBS, DHC | Midland/Scottish |
| 105 | LD | DMBS, DMC, DTC | Eastern |
| 107 | LD | DMBS, DMS, TS | Scottish |
| 108 | LD | DMBS, DMC, DTC, TBS, TS | Midland/Eastern |
| 110 | LD | DMBC, DMC, TS | Eastern |
| 111 | LD | DMBS, DMC, DHBS, DHC | Eastern |
| 114 | LD | DMBS, DTC | Eastern |
| 115 | HD | DMBS, TC, TS | Midland |
| 116 | HD | DMBS, DMS, TS | Midland/Eastern/Western/Scottish |
| 117 | HD | DMBS, DMS, TC | Western |
| 118 | HD | DMBS, DMS, TC | Western |
| 119 | CC | DMBC, DMS, TS | Western |
| 120 | CC | DMBS, DMC, DMBF, TS | Midland/Western |
| 121 | HD | DMBS, DTS | Western |
| 122 | HD | DMBS | Midland |
| 127 | HD | TS | Midland |
| 128 | PCLS | DMLV | Midland/Western |
| 140 | HD | DMS, DMSL | Western |
| 141 | HD | DMS, DMSL | Eastern |
| 142 | HD | DMS, DMSL | Midland/Western |
| 143 | HD | DMS, DMSL | |
| 150 | HD | DMS, MS | Midland |
| 151 | HD | DMS, MS | Midland |
| 201 (6S) | LD | DMBS, TC, TS | Southern |
| 202 (6L) | LD | DMBS, TC, TS | Southern |
| 203 (5L) | LD | DMBS, TC, TS | Southern |
| 204 (3T) | HD | DMBS, DTC, TS | Southern |
| 205 (3H) | HD | DMBS, DTC, TS | Southern |
| 207 (3D) | HD | DMBS, DTS, TC | Southern |
| 210 | LD | DMBS, DMS, DTS, TC, TS | Western |
| 253 | HST | DM, TF, TGS, TRSB, TRUB, TS | Western/Midland |
| 254 | HST | DM, DMB, TF, TGS, TRSB, TRUB, TRUK, TFLK, TS | Eastern/Scottish |

Note: The column headed 'Car Types' lists all types in service under the classification but these will not always be found operating within the same train formation.

**Late information**

In late 1985 orders were placed for further new DMU sets for delivery from 1986 onwards, including:

**Class 142/1** units Nos 142.101-146 formed DMBS 55701-46, DMS(L) 55747-92 (Leyland/BREL);

**Class 144** units Nos 144.001-023 formed DMS 55801-23, DMS(L) 55824-46 (W. Alexander/BREL);

**Class 150/2** units Nos 150.201-285 formed DMS(L) 52201-85, DMS 57201-85 (BREL);

**Class 155** units Nos 155.301-335 formed DMS(L) 52301-35, DMS 57301-35 (Leyland);

**Class 156** units Nos 156.401-514 formed DMS(L) 52401-514, DMS 57401-514 (Metro-Cammell).

All new 'Sprinter' units are expected to be fitted with inter-unit corridor gangways. The Class 155 and 156 vehicles are to have 23m length bodies in place of the previous 20m standard length.

# Liveries & Logos

Before 1967 all diesel unit stock was outshopped in green livery with numbers and lettering usually applied in yellow. Visibility warning ends started to appear in the early 1960s, firstly as panels but gradually growing in size until the full yellow end was adopted as standard from around 1966.

By late 1966 the Railways Board were keen to promote their new corporate image and this resulted in the introduction of revised liveries for all stock. Main line trains were given a two-tone grey/blue scheme, whilst suburban vehicles were outshopped in all-over rail blue livery. Generally full yellow ends were applied from the introduction of the blue scheme; some of the earliest blue stock did emerge with small yellow panels but this only lasted for a short period. All-over blue was progressively applied to all diesel units except 'Cross-Country', 'Trans-Pennine' and 'Inter-City' sets which emerged in the main line grey/blue colours.

These schemes remained unchanged until the early 1970s when it was decided that the drab all-over blue carried by the majority of units would be altered. The SR 'Hastings' units were repainted in blue/grey colours and a number of mechanical sets were outshopped in an off-white colour with a wide blue waist band; whilst this looked aesthetically pleasing it was a nightmare to keep clean and after only a short period the stock liveries were again reviewed. This time it was decided to paint all stock in the blue/grey colours except those scheduled for early withdrawal. In early 1985 the only remaining all blue stock was from Classes 100, 104 and 105. In recent years a number of areas have re-painted stock in localised colours, usually associated with Passenger Transport Executives (PTE). This has also led to a number of PTE logos being applied to stock, some of which are illustrated below. The most striking livery variant is the orange/black applied to some Scottish sets, and one Class 114 unit to which South Yorkshire PTE brown/cream livery has been applied.

Following the introduction of the new Classes 141, 142, 143, 150 and 151 sets, again new colour schemes appeared. The Class 141, originally blue/grey, were re-painted after only a few months in a green/cream livery, whilst the Class 142 units have appeared in Manchester PTE orange and WR chocolate & cream. The Class 143, as this book went to press, was completed in a blue/white scheme, while the Class 150 carry an all-over grey scheme with a broad blue band at window height and a white/light blue band below. The Metro-Cammell built Class 151s probably carry the most striking finish decorated in aluminium and blue.

In early 1985 BR entered into a joint advertising campaign with British Telecom, culminating in a Class 118 being painted in Telecom yellow and adorned with advertising slogans and pictures. The unit was due to be repainted into standard colours in early 1986.

To mark the GWR150 celebrations on the Western Region some of the Region's DMU stock appeared in mock GWR livery.

Left:
*Following the formation of a number of Passenger Transport Executives (PTE) and the introduction of local fleet names, a number of different liveries and logos were applied to vehicles. The four logos shown here — South Yorkshire, West Yorkshire, Greater Manchester and Tyne & Wear PTE, are displayed at Doncaster Works for the guidance of painting staff.*
Michael J. Collins

# Class 100

**Car Type:** DMBS
**Car Numbers:** 53355
**Former Numbers:** 50355
**Introduced:** 1957
**Built by:** Gloucester RCW
**Engine Manufacturer:** AEC
**Horsepower (total):** 300
**Weight of Car:** 30.5 tonnes
**Length over Body:** 17.52m
**Height of Car:** 3.87m
**Width of Car:** 2.81m
**Brake Type:** Vacuum
**Maximum Speed:** 70mph (113km/hr)
**Internal Layout:** Low density
**Seating:** 52 Second
**Region of Allocation:** LMR
**Depot of Allocation:** NH
**Works responsible for overhauls:**
None scheduled

Below:
*The once sizeable Class 100 fleet is now reduced to just one vehicle — DMBS No 53355, allocated to Newton Heath. This car is quite distinctive amongst the DMMU fleet, the most noticeable frontal recognition factor being the yellow painted area extending down the sides of the buffer beam. This is a low density type vehicle seating 52 second class passengers and is scheduled for early withdrawal. No 53355 is seen at Rotherham leading an empty stock train from Doncaster works to Newton Heath during 1984.* Colin J. Marsden

# Class 101

| | | |
|---|---|---|
| **Car Type:** | DMC | DMBS |
| **Car Numbers:** | 51495-51539 | 51174-51253 |
| | 51802-51808 | 51425-51470 |
| | 53138-53151 | 51795-51801 |
| | 53158-53163 | 53153-53157 |
| | 53168-53197 | 53164-53167 |
| | 53234-53245 | 53198-53233 |
| | 53260-53269 | 53246-53259 |
| | 53321-53338 | 53290-53320 |
| | 53746-53751 | — |
| **Former Numbers:** | 50138-50151 | 50153-50157 |
| | 50158-50163 | 50164-50167 |
| | 50168-50197 | 50198-50233 |
| | 50234-50245 | 50246-50259 |
| | 50260-50269 | 50290-50320 |
| | 50321-50338 | — |
| | 50746-50751 | — |
| **Introduced:** | 1956-59 | 1956-59 |
| **Built by:** | Metro-Cammell | Metro-Cammell |
| **Engine Manufacturer:** | Leyland | Leyland |
| **Horsepower (total):** | 300 | 300 |
| **Weight of Car:** | 32.5 tonnes | 32.5 tonnes |
| **Length over Body:** | 17.37m | 17.37m |
| **Height of Car:** | 3.77m | 3.77m |
| **Width of Car:** | 2.81m | 2.81m |
| **Brake Type:** | Vacuum | Vacuum |
| **Maximum Speed:** | 70mph (113km/hr) | 70mph (113km/hr) |
| **Internal Layout:** | Low density | Low density |
| **Seating:** | 45 Second,* 12 First | 52 Second* |
| **Regions of Allocation:** | ER, LMR, WR, ScR | LMR, WR, ScR |
| **Depots of Allocation:** | AY, CF, CH, ED, HA, HT, NC, NL | AY, BG, CA, CF, CH, ED, HA, NT, NC, NL, TS |
| **Works responsible for overhauls:** | Glasgow, Derby, Swindon, Doncaster | Glasgow, Derby, Swindon, Doncaster |
| | * Some seat 12 First, 53 Second ER, LMR cars declassified — 65 Second | * Some seat 44 Second |

Right:
*The Class 101 sets are low density units with on average two passenger doors on each side of vehicles. There are two types of power car within the Class 101: Driving Motor Composite (DMC) and Driving Motor Brake Second (DMBS). The DMC has the two bays directly behind the cab for first class occupation, with the remainder of the vehicle for second class passengers, with a toilet at the inner end. DMC No 50240 now 53240 is illustrated at Ipswich. Note: A number of DMC vehicles are downgraded and classified Driving Motor Second (DMS).* Colin J. Marsden

| DTC | TS | TBS | TC |
|---|---|---|---|
| 54050-54093 | 59042-59048 | 59049-59055 | 59114-59131 |
| 54218-54220 | 59060-59072 | 59073-59085 | 59523-59568 |
| 54332-54411 | 59086-59091 | 59092-59097 | — |
| — | 59100-59108 | 59112-59113 | — |
| — | 59302-59306 | — | — |
| — | 59569-59572 | — | — |
| — | 59686-59692 | — | — |
| — | — | — | — |
| — | — | — | — |
| 56050-56093 | — | — | — |
| 56218-56220 | — | — | — |
| 56332-56411 | — | — | — |
| — | — | — | — |
| — | — | — | — |
| — | — | — | — |
| — | — | — | — |
| 1957-58 | 1956-59 | 1956-58 | 1958-59 |
| Metro-Cammell | Metro-Cammell | Metro-Cammell | Metro-Cammell |
| — | — | — | — |
| — | — | — | — |
| 26.5 tonnes | 25.5 tonnes | 25.5 tonnes | 25.5 tonnes |
| 17.37m | 17.37m | 17.37m | 17.37m |
| 3.77m | 3.77m | 3.77m | 3.77m |
| 2.81m | 2.81m | 2.81m | 2.81m |
| Vacuum | Vacuum | Vacuum | Vacuum |
| 70mph (113km/hr) | 70mph (113km/hr) | 70mph (113km/hr) | 70mph (113km/hr) |
| Low density | Low density | Low density | Low density |
| 45 Second, 12 First* | Between 61-71 Second* | Between 45-65 Second* | 53 Second, 12 First* |
| ER, LMR | LMR, ScR | ER, LMR, WR, ScR | ER, LMR, WR, ScR |
| BG, CA, CH, HT, NC, NL | AY, CH, DY, ED, HA, NH, TS | AY, BG, CF, CH, HA, HT, NC, NH | BR, CF, CH, DY, ED, HA, NC, NH, RG, TS |
| Derby, Doncaster | Glasgow, Derby, | Glasgow, Derby, Swindon, Doncaster | Glasgow, Derby, Swindon Doncaster |
| * Some seat 53 Second<br><br>ER, LMR cars declassified — 57 Second | * Depending on build | * Depending on build | * Some declassified — 65 Second |

Top:
*The Class 101 DMBS vehicle is illustrated here by car No 51437. Behind the driving cab are four rows of forward facing seats with a central gangway, being followed by a transverse walkway and further bus-style seating, before another transverse walkway with a guard's and luggage compartment beyond. Underslung between the bogies on both DMC and DMBS cars are two Leyland 150hp engines, gearbox, final drive, heating and battery boxes.* Colin J. Marsden

Above:
*To operate with DMBS cars and forming 2-car sets, a fleet of Driving Trailer Composite (DTC) vehicles was constructed. These are identical to the DMC except that no power equipment is carried; this is easily recognised by the lack of underframe equipment. These DTCs are all allocated to the Eastern and Midland Regions and the majority are now declassified seating only second class passengers and thus termed as DTS. Car No 54378 is illustrated.* Colin J. Marsden

Top:
*To permit the formation of 3-car sets, three types of intermediate trailer were constructed, the most numerous being the Trailer Second (TS). These vehicles have three access doors on each side with a toilet at one end. The total seating capacity varies between 61 and 71, depending on build. The 3-car set illustrated is formed: DMBS, TS, DMS.* Colin J. Marsden

Above:
*A total of 27 Trailer Brake Second (TBS) cars are in service, allocated to all regions having Class 101s. These vehicles are basically a TS with a guard's office and luggage area at one end. Two passenger doors are positioned on each side and seating is provided for 45-65 passengers, again depending on build. Underfloor mounted equipment consists mainly of heating, lighting and brake modules. Car No 59097 is illustrated at Ipswich.* Colin J. Marsden

Below:
*Allocated to each Class 101 operating region are Trailer Composite (TC) vehicles. These are again based on the TS style body with two seating bays at one end devoted to first class patronage, seating being arranged in the 2+1 style. Underfloor equipment is the same as on the TBS. WR allocated No 59550 is shown.* Colin J. Marsden

Bottom:
*Scottish Region 3-car Class 101 in action: Sets on ScR are allocated to Ayr, Eastfield and Haymarket and operate along with Class 107/116s on the majority of non-electrified suburban services. Set No 101.305 formed DMBS, TS, DMC departs from Edinburgh bound for Glasgow in 1984.* Colin J. Marsden

Below:
*The ER has Class 101 vehicles of all types except TS on their books, thus 2- and 3-car formations are possible. A 2-car set with a DMBS leading departs from Knottingley in 1983 on a Goole working.* Colin J. Marsden

Bottom:
*Today is the age of livery variants and the Class 101 has not escaped the painter's attention. This Tyseley allocated 3-car set formed DMC (De-classified to DTS), TS, DMBS has black cab window surrounds to the standard blue/grey livery which, in the author's opinion, enhances the unit's appearance.* Colin J. Marsden

# Class 104

| Car Type: | DMBS | DMC | DTC |
|---|---|---|---|
| **Car Numbers:** | 53420-53422 | 53424-53427 | 54175-54189 |
| | 53428-53479 | 53482-53531 | — |
| | 53532-53541 | 53542-53593 | — |
| | 53594-53598 | — | — |
| **Former Numbers:** | 50420-50422 | 50424-50427 | 56175-56189 |
| | 50428-50479 | 50482-50531 | — |
| | 50532-50541 | 50542-50593 | — |
| | 50594-50598 | — | — |
| **Introduced:** | 1957-58 | 1957 | 1958 |
| **Built by:** | BRCW | BRCW | BRCW |
| **Engine Manufacturer:** | Leyland | Leyland | — |
| **Horsepower (total):** | 300 | 300 | — |
| **Weight of Car:** | 31.5 tonnes | 31.5 tonnes | 24.5 tonnes |
| **Length over Body:** | 17.52m | 17.52m | 17.52m |
| **Height of Car:** | 3.87m | 3.87m | 3.87m |
| **Width of Car:** | 2.81m | 2.81m | 2.81m |
| **Brake Type:** | Vacuum | Vacuum | Vacuum |
| **Maximum Speed:** | 70mph (113km/hr) | 70mph (113km/hr) | 70mph (113km/hr) |
| **Internal Layout:** | Low density | Low density | Low density |
| **Seating:** | 52 Second | 54 Second, 12 First* | 54 Second, 12 First* |
| **Regions of Allocation:** | Midland, Scottish | Midland, Scottish | Midland |
| **Depots of Allocation:** | AY, BX, BY, CW, ED, NH | AY, BX, BY, CW, ED, NH | BY, NH |
| **Works responsible for overhauls:** | Derby, Glasgow | Derby, Glasgow | Derby |

* Some seated 51 Second, 12 First. All declassified — 63 Second or 66 Second

† All declassified — 66 Second

Below:
*These BRCW Class 104 units of which there are eight different vehicle types, are scheduled for withdrawal at an early opportunity. Two Power Car types exist — DMBS and DMC. The DMBS is illustrated here. These cars are similar to the Class 101 DMBS with seating, windows and doors in the same positions. The front end is largely different with taller windows and a route destination box in the roof rather than on the front end. Car No 53595 is illustrated at Walsall.* Colin J. Marsden

| TC | TS | TBS | DHBS | DHC |
|---|---|---|---|---|
| 59137-59187 | 59195-59207 | 59210-59228 | 78851 | 78601 |
| — | 59230 | — | — | — |
| — | — | — | — | — |
| — | — | — | — | — |
| — | — | — | — | — |
| — | — | — | 50446 | 50521 |
| — | — | — | — | — |
| — | — | — | — | — |
| 1957 | 1958 | 1958 | 1957 | 1957 |
| BRCW | BRCW | BRCW | BRCW | BRCW |
| — | — | — | Leyland | Leyland |
| — | — | — | 150 | 150 |
| 22.5 tonnes | 22.5 tonnes | 23.5 tonnes | 30.5 tonnes | 30.5 tonnes |
| 17.52m | 17.52m | 17.52. | 17.52m | 17.52m |
| 3.87m | 3.87m | 3.87m | 3.87m | 3.87m |
| 2.81m | 2.81m | 2.81m | 2.81m | 2.81m |
| Vacuum | Vacuum | Vacuum | Vacuum | Vacuum |
| 70mph (113km/hr) | 70mph (113km/hr) | 70mph (113km/hr) | 70mph (113km/hr) | 70mph (113km/hr) |
| Low density | Low density | Low density | Low density | Low density |
| 54 Second, 12 First† | 68 Second | 50 Second | 52 Second | 54 Second, 12 First† |
| Midland | Midland | Scottish, Midland | Midland | Midland |
| BX, BY, NH | BX, BY | AY, BX | LO | LO |
| Derby | Derby | Glasgow, Derby | Doncaster | Doncaster |

Below:
*To operate at the opposite end of the train to Motor Brake vehicles were two forms of composite vehicle — Driving Motor Composite and Driving Trailer Composite. These cars are identical except for power equipment on the DMCs. Seating is provided for 54 second and 12 first class passengers, however today most cars have their first class accommodation declassified, thus they should correctly be classified DMS or DTS. Two DMC(S) cars stand side by side at Buxton. Note the car on the left retains a ventilation grille under the Assistant's window.* Colin J. Marsden

Top:
*Class 104 stock in original condition. When introduced these sets were in all-over green livery with a white cab roof area. A yellow strip was applied under the side windows and along the front end just below cab window height. Two Class 104s stand at Stoke Cockshute depot in October 1957.* BR

Above:
*Three different intermediate Trailer vehicles exist within this Class, all based on the same body design. The BRCW Trailer vehicles are always immediately recognisable by having large windows adjacent to the corridor connections. The TS type is illustrated, having three access doors on either side and a toilet at the far end. TC vehicles are the same style with a two-bay compartment at one end, laid out for first class occupants, opposite the toilet. TBS cars have guards and luggage facilities at one end occupying the space of two seating bays. TS No 59230 is illustrated.* Colin J. Marsden

Top:
*During 1982 two LMR allocated Class 104 cars, DMBS No 50446 and DMC No 50521, were rebuilt at BREL Doncaster and experimentally re-equipped with single engines (developing 150hp). Externally the vehicles were the same as conventional cars except for the space on the underframe from where the engine was removed and a black strip applied under the front windows, together with the legend EXP DM352. — meaning Experiment-Diesel Mechanical 352, thus indicating to operating staff the single engine modification. After release to the LM it was decided to renumber single engine cars in the 7XXXX range and reclassify the vehicles DHBS and DHC. No 50521 which became 78601 is illustrated; this car was declassified and is thus officially a DHS.* Derek Porter

Above:
*The Class 104s are allocated to the LMR except for a handful which operate on the Scottish Region. A Power Twin, formed of a DMBS and DMC approaches Upper Holloway with a Gospel Oak-Barking train.* Colin J. Marsden

# Class 105

**Car Type:** DMBS
**Car Numbers:** 51259-51299
51472-51478
53359-53381
**Former Numbers:** 50359-50387

**Introduced:** 1956-59
**Built by:** Cravens
**Engine Manufacturer:** Leyland
**Horsepower (total):** 300
**Weight of Car:** 29.5 tonnes
**Length over Body:** 17.53m
**Height of Car:** 3.83m
**Width of Car:** 2.81m
**Brake Type:** Vacuum
**Maximum Speed:** 70mph (113km/hr)
**Internal Layout:** Low density
**Seating:** 52 Second
**Regions of Allocation:** Eastern
**Depots of Allocation:** LN, NC, SF
**Works responsible for overhauls:** Doncaster

Above:
*There are three vehicle types within the Class 105, all are driving cars and thus formations are confined to 2-car sets. The front design of this stock leaves them immediately recognisable amongst the DMMU fleet, the most noticeable front feature being the two square windows and the destination indicator above, which has the gutter rail drop away on either side. A DMBS is the leading vehicle in this picture.*
Colin J. Marsden

| DMC | DTC |
|---|---|
| 53812 | 54114-54143 |
| — | 54416-54472 |
| — | — |
| 50812 | 56114-56143 |
| — | 56416-56472 |
| 1957 | 1956-58 |
| Cravens | Cravens |
| Leyland | — |
| 300 | — |
| 30.5 tonnes | 23.5 tonnes |
| 17.53m | 17.53m |
| 3.83m | 3.83m |
| 2.81m | 2.81m |
| Vacuum | Vacuum |
| 70mph (113km/hr) | 70mph (113km/hr) |
| Low density | Low density |
| 51 Second, 12 First* | 51 Second, 12 First† |
| Midland | Eastern |
| NH | LN, NC, SF |
| Doncaster | Doncaster |

* Declassified — 63 Second

† Some declassified — 63 Second

Above:
*The internal layout of these vehicles is very similar to those previously dealt with. Two passenger access doors are located on either side of DMBS cars, and bus-style seating is provided adjacent to two large side windows directly behind the cab, with three windows in the centre of the coach. A small guard's compartment and luggage cage are provided at the inner end. Car No 53784 (now withdrawn) is nearest the camera in this view taken at Windermere.* Colin J. Marsden

Below:
*The one surviving member of the DMC fleet No 53812 has had its first class accommodation declassified, and is thus a DMS vehicle. This car has two passenger doors on each side feeding a transverse walkway, giving access to 63 seats in total. Those directly behind the cab being the former first class, and are in the 2+1 style, whilst the remainder is in bus-style.* Colin J. Marsden

Below:
*Driving Trailer Composite (DTC) cars were built to enable 2-car (one powered) formations to operate. These vehicles are identical to the DMC cars, except for the omission of traction equipment. DTC No 54133 pulls into Camden Road with a Woolwich shuttle in 1984. Some DTC vehicles have been declassified and thus seat 63 second class passengers and are classified DTS.* Colin J. Marsden

Above:
*All Class 105 units retain all-over blue livery and some have gained white cab roofs, particularly those operating in the London area, while others have acquired two headlights. The allocation today is shared between LN, NC, NH and SF. A 2-car set formed DMBS, DTC stops at Caledonian Road & Barnsbury with a Woolwich-Camden Road train on 6 June 1984.* Colin J. Marsden

Left:
*Coupling: this plate shows the coupling between the two coaches of a Class 105 unit, the train control and train braking pipes are connected via flexible pipes below, whilst two 'Pullman'-style gangways make the passenger connection. The pipe running down the left coach is the toilet water tank overflow pipe, whilst the handles at cant rail height on each coach are the resets for the passenger communication equipment.* Colin J. Marsden

# Class 107

| Car Type: | DMBS | DMS |
|---|---|---|
| Car Numbers: | 51985-52010 | 52011-52036 |
| Former Numbers: | — | — |
| Introduced: | 1960 | 1960 |
| Built by: | BR Derby | BR Derby |
| Engine Manufacturer: | Leyland | Leyland |
| Horsepower (total): | 300 | 300 |
| Weight of Car: | 35 tonnes | 35.5 tonnes |
| Length over Body: | 17.7m | 17.7m |
| Height of Car: | 3.77m | 3.77m |
| Width of Car: | 2.81m | 2.81m |
| Brake Type: | Vacuum | Vacuum |
| Maximum Speed: | 70mph (113km/hr) | 70mph (113km/hr) |
| Internal Layout: | Low density | Low density |
| Seating: | 52 Second | 65 Second |
| Region of Allocation: | Scottish | Scottish |
| Depot of Allocation: | AY | AY |
| Works responsible for overhauls: | Glasgow | Glasgow |

Above:
*A large number of DMMU sets were constructed by BR Derby Works during the late 1950s-early 1960s, the majority of these look identical but detail differences do exist. The 25 members of Class 107 are all 3-car sets and are allocated to the Scottish Region. The DMBS vehicle is depicted here: two passenger doors are provided on each side, giving access to 52 seats. A guard's office and luggage van are at the inner end. DMBS No 51993 leads in this view.* John Tuffs

Above right:
*The DMS cars are similar to the DMBS vehicles but the guard's/luggage area is omitted and a total of 65 seats provided. To operate between the power cars a fleet of TS vehicles were built. These have three passenger doors per side, and seating is arranged in three sections. There is a toilet at one end. Underslung equipment consists of heating, lighting, braking and battery units. Set No 107.449 with DTS No 52034 leading, stands at Kilwinning on 9 August 1982. John Tuffs*

TS
59782-59807
—
1960
BR Derby
—
—
28.5 tonnes
17.7m
3.77m
2.81m
Vacuum
70mph (113km/hr)
Low density
71 Second
Scottish
AY
Glasgow

Bottom:
*Although the majority of Class 107 units are painted in conventional blue/grey livery, a few have been outshopped in a Strathclyde Transport orange and black scheme, together with a black front window surround. Revised liveried set No 107.444 with its DMBS leading stands at Edinburgh in late 1984. All Scottish allocated units carry their six-digit unit numbers, but this should not be relied upon for individual vehicle identification as car changes regularly take place.* Colin J. Marsden

# Class 108

| | | |
|---|---|---|
| **Car Type:** | DMBS | DMC |
| **Car Numbers:** | 51416-51424 | 51561-51572 |
| | 51901-51950 | 52037-52065 |
| | 53599-53629 | 53630-53646 |
| | 53924-53987 | — |
| **Former Numbers:** | 50599-50629 | 50630-50646 |
| | 50924-50987 | — |
| | — | — |
| **Introduced:** | 1958-60 | 1958-60 |
| **Built by:** | BR Derby | BR Derby |
| **Engine Manufacturer:** | Leyland | Leyland |
| **Horsepower (total):** | 300 | 300 |
| **Weight of Car:** | 29.5 tonnes | 29.5 tonnes |
| **Length over Body:** | 17.7m | 17.7m |
| **Height of Car:** | 3.77m | 3.77m |
| **Width of Car:** | 2.81m | 2.81m |
| **Brake Type:** | Vacuum | Vacuum |
| **Maximum Speed:** | 70mph (113km/hr) | 70mph (113km/hr) |
| **Internal Layout:** | Low density | Low density |
| **Seating:** | 52 Second | 53 Second 12 First* |
| **Regions of Allocation:** | Midland, Eastern, | Midland, Eastern |
| **Depots of Allocation:** | AN, BG, BX, CH, KD, NH, NL | AN, BG, BX, CH, NH |
| **Works responsible for overhauls:** | Derby, Doncaster | Derby, Doncaster |

* Some seat 50 Second, 12 First. All declassified † All declassified

Above:
*At a casual glance the Class 108 units look very similar to the Class 107s, also being built by BR Derby. Probably the easiest way of quick recognition is that a small roof-mounted destination indicator is carried on most Class 108s, whereas a four-position route indicator box is fitted to the Class 107s. Class 108 DMBS No 50968, now renumbered 53968, is seen at Preston in 1980.* Colin J. Marsden

Note: Some members of the final Class 108 batch are equipped with four-position route boxes.

| DTC | TBS | TS |
|---|---|---|
| 54190-54214 | 59245-59250 | 59380-59390 |
| 54221-54279 | — | — |
| 54484-54504 | — | — |
| — | — | — |
| 56190-56214 | — | — |
| 56221-56279 | — | — |
| 56484-56504 | — | — |
| 1958-60 | 1958 | 1958 |
| BR Derby | BR Derby | BR Derby |
| — | — | — |
| — | — | — |
| 21.5 tonnes | 23.5 tonnes | 22.5 tonnes |
| 17.7m | 17.7m | 17.7m |
| 3.77m | 3.77m | 3.77m |
| 2.81m | 2.81m | 2.81m |
| Vacuum | Vacuum | Vacuum |
| 70mph (113km/hr) | 70mph (113km/hr) | 70mph (113km/hr) |
| Low density | Low density | Low density |
| 53 Second 12 First† | 50 Second | 68 Second |
| Midland, Eastern | Eastern | Midland, Eastern |
| AN, BG, CH, KD, NH, NL | BG | BG, BX |
| Derby, Doncaster | Doncaster | Derby, Doncaster |

Below:
*In addition to the DMBS fleet, a number of DMC power vehicles were built for Class 108; closely resembling the Class 107 DMS stock. Class 108 DMCs have now been declassified to second class only occupation and reclassified DMS. Underframe and buffer beam equipment is of the standard pattern with accommodation for 52 passengers. A DMC painted in all-over blue livery stands at Doncaster prior to the abolition of first class accommodation on South Yorkshire services.* Colin J. Marsden

Top:
*When built the Class 108 Driving vehicles that did not incorporate a four-position roof indicator, had a two digit headcode panel under the centre front window, but these have all now been removed. There are few detail differences within the fleet but a number of Driving cars allocated to the Midland for use in the North-West have barred windows to prevent passengers leaning out of windows. A DTC declassified to DTS is seen with barred windows at Workington.* Colin J. Marsden

Above:
*A fleet of six Trailer Brake Second (TBS) vehicles for Class 108 were built in 1958 and all are now allocated to Botanic Gardens depot. These seat 50 passengers, have a toilet at one end, and a guard's office/luggage area at the other. This illustration shows a 4-car Class 108 near York with a TBS as the second vehicle.* Colin J. Marsden

Bottom left:
*A fleet of 11 Class 108 Trailer Seconds was introduced in 1958 and these are now allocated to BG and BX depots. Each coach has accommodation for 68 with toilets at one end; three passenger access doors being provided on each side. Although the vehicle illustrated, No 59381, is in white/blue livery, all are presently in the blue/grey scheme.* Brian Morrison

Above and right:
*The Class 108 fleet are now all painted in blue/grey livery and operate on the London Midland and Eastern regions. In the first illustration a 2-car set led by a DTS approaches Carnforth with a service from Barrow, while the following plate shows 2-car set Nos 54259/53941 at Romiley Junction with the 13.27 New Mills Central-Manchester Piccadilly on 11 July 1984.* Colin J. Marsden/John Tuffs

# Class 110

| Car Type: | DMBC | DMC |
|---|---|---|
| Car Numbers: | 51809-51828<br>52066-52075 | 51829-51847<br>52076-52085 |
| Former Numbers: | — | — |
| Introduced: | 1961 | 1961 |
| Built by: | BRCW | BRCW |
| Engine Manufacturer: | Rolls-Royce | Rolls-Royce |
| Horsepower (total): | 360 | 360 |
| Weight of Car: | 33.5 tonnes | 33 tonnes |
| Length over Body: | 17.53m | 17.53m |
| Height of Car: | 3.88m | 3.88m |
| Width of Car: | 2.81m | 2.81m |
| Brake Type: | Vacuum | Vacuum |
| Maximum Speed: | 70mph (113km/hr) | 70mph (113km/hr) |
| Internal Layout: | Low density | Low density |
| Seating: | 33 Second, 12 First* | 54 Second, 12 First* |
| Region of Allocation: | Eastern | Eastern |
| Depot of Allocation: | NL | NL |
| Works responsible for overhauls: | Doncaster | Doncaster |

* Declassified — 45 Second

Above:
*Probably the most distinctive of the DMMU types presently in service are the Birmingham RC&W constructed Class 110, with their slanting top driver's windows, with a smaller centre panel and destination indicator above. There was a four-position route indicator on the roof but these are no longer in use and have been plated over. The DMBC type vehicle is illustrated. Note that the warning horns are under each buffer, unusual on DMU stock.* Colin J. Marsden

Top right:
*There are two types of power driving vehicle within the Class 110, the DMBC and the DMC. They are basically the same except that on DMBC coaches 21 seats at the inner end are lost where the guard's accommodation is situated. DMC No 51844 is illustrated on the outskirts of York. All first class accommodation on these sets has now been removed and thus vehicles have been reclassified as DMBS/DMS.* Colin J. Marsden

TS
59694-59710
59809-59817
—
1961
BRCW
—
—
25.5 tonnes
17.53m
3.88m
2.81m
Vacuum
70mph (113km/hr)
Low density
72 Second
Eastern
NL
Doncaster

Below:
*The Class 110 can either operate as power twins (developing 720hp) or as 3-car formations with the addition of a TS accommodating 72 passengers. These cars, like the Class 104, have windows adjacent to the corridor connection. Minor detail differences exist between them, mainly the positioning of end windows and the seating. TS No 59811 is illustrated in Doncaster Works painted in white/blue livery. Recognition between the two TS types is best achieved by reference to the number.*
Colin J. Marsden

Above:
*Two separate batches of Class 110 units were built, but few detail differences exist between them. However, one front alteration was made — the fitting of grab rails under and adjacent to the nose windows to the second batch of Driving Car, but some of these have now been removed. A 3-car set led by DMC(S) No 52077 is seen at Naburn with a York-Doncaster local on 6 July 1983 before the route via Selby was abolished.*
Colin J. Marsden

Left:
*The Class 110s are often referred to as the 'Calder Valley sets' after the route they usually operate over, however the operating range is more widespread today, all are allocated to Leeds Neville Hill depot. Photographed during the livery transition period a 3-car set with two blue/grey and one all-blue coach, approaches Brightside with a Leeds-Manchester service on 10 September 1981.* Colin J. Marsden

Above:
*Class 110 front end detail. The buffer beam equipment is the same as detailed for Class 101, except for the positioning of the air horns. Note how the former headcode box has been crudely welded up; the car illustrated is No 52075.* Colin J. Marsden

# Class 111

| | | |
|---|---|---|
| **Car Type:** | DMBS | DHC |
| **Car Numbers:** | 53134-53137 | 78706-78724 |
| | — | — |
| **Former Numbers:** | 50134-51037 | 51551-51560 |
| | — | 53271-53279 |
| | | (not in order) |
| **Introduced:** | 1957-59 | 1957-59 |
| **Built by:** | Metro-Cammell | Metro-Cammell |
| **Engine Manufacturer:** | Rolls-Royce | Rolls-Royce |
| **Horsepower (total):** | 360 | 180 |
| **Weight of Car:** | 33.5 tonnes | 32.5 tonnes |
| **Length over Body:** | 17.53m | 17.53m |
| **Height of Car:** | 3.77m | 3.77m |
| **Width of Car:** | 2.81m | 2.81m |
| **Brake Type:** | Vacuum | Vacuum |
| **Maximum Speed:** | 70mph (113km/hr) | 70mph (113km/hr) |
| **Internal Layout:** | Low density | Low density |
| **Seating:** | 52 Second | 53 Second, 12 First* |
| **Region of Allocation:** | Eastern | Eastern |
| **Depot of Allocation:** | NL | NL |
| **Works responsible for overhauls:** | Doncaster | Doncaster |

* Declassified — 64 Second

Above:
*A fleet of 49 Metro-Cammell sets was introduced between 1957-59 powered by Rolls-Royce engines, developing 360hp. Their body design was identical to that of Class 101 and recognition between the two types is not easy. Some of the later built cars are marginally different, incorporating the destination indicator slightly recessed into the centre window line. A DMC vehicle No 51555 is illustrated departing from Doncaster.*
Colin J. Marsden

DHBS
78956-78974
—
51541-51550
53280-53289
(not in order)
1957-59
Metro-Cammell
Rolls-Royce
180
32.5 tonnes
17.53m
3.77m
2.81m
Vacuum
70mph (113km/hr)
Low density
52 Second
Eastern
NL
Doncaster

Above:
*All Class 111 units are scheduled for single engine modification, but at the time of writing, some double engine examples are still in service. All vehicles are allocated to Neville Hill and usually operate in the South Yorkshire PTE area. To assist with recognition of the Class 101/111 types throughout the country, it is unlikely that Class 111 sets will be seen away from the ER. A 2-car set approaches York with a train from Doncaster.* Colin J. Marsden

Below:
*During the early 1980s it was decided as a cost saving measure, that Class 111 power cars would lose one of their engines, reducing each car to 180hp. However as it was intended to operate two power cars together this gave no significant loss of traction output. Vehicles so treated have been renumbered in the 7XXXX range. Exterior recognition is best achieved by reference to the number, but a space can be seen on the underframe where the power unit was formerly located. The vehicle illustrated, No 78966, is a DHBS (formerly a DMBS) and is shown from the guard's end.*
Colin J. Marsden

# Class 114

| | | |
|---|---|---|
| **Car Type:** | DMBS | DTC |
| **Car Numbers:** | 53001-53047 | 54001-54047 |
| **Former Numbers:** | 50001-50047 | 56001-56047 |
| **Introduced:** | 1956 | 1956 |
| **Built by:** | BR Derby | BR Derby |
| **Engine Manufacturer:** | Leyland Albion | — |
| **Horsepower (total):** | 400 | — |
| **Weight of Car:** | 38 tonnes | 30 tonnes |
| **Length over Body:** | 19.66m | 19.66m |
| **Height of Car:** | 3.77m | 3.77m |
| **Width of Car:** | 2.81m | 2.81m |
| **Brake Type:** | Vacuum | Vacuum |
| **Maximum Speed:** | 70mph (113km/hr) | 70mph (113km/hr) |
| **Internal Layout:** | Low density | Low density |
| **Seating:** | 62 Second | 62 Second, 12 First* |
| **Region of Allocation:** | Eastern | Eastern |
| **Depot of Allocation:** | LN | LN |
| **Works responsible for overhauls:** | Doncaster | Doncaster |

* Now declassified — 74 Second

Above:
*This fleet of ER allocated Class 114s are another Derby product and are similar to Class 107, 108 stock. However these are 'heavyweight' sets, being built on long frames, and therefore have an additional side window between the two passenger doors; there is a toilet provided at the inner end. A DTC declassified to DTS is illustrated, leading a Cleethorpes train into Rotherham.* Colin J. Marsden

Above:
*Power cars for the Class 114 fleet are provided in the shape of Driving Motor Brake Seconds. Again these are very similar to comparable vehicles of Classes 107/108 but are recognisable by their long frame. A 2-car set with its DMBS leading departs from Doncaster bound for Sleaford on 31 August 1982.* Colin J. Marsden

Below:
*All Class 114s are allocated to Lincoln depot and usually operate on South Yorkshire and Lincolnshire duties. Today all but one set are painted in conventional blue/grey livery. The 17.55 Sheffield-Sleaford led by DTS No 54008, passes Kiverton Park Colliery on 30 June 1983.* Colin J. Marsden

# Class 115

| | | |
|---|---|---|
| **Car Type:** | DMBS | TS |
| **Car Numbers:** | 51651-51680<br>51849-51900<br>— | 59649-59663<br>59713-59717<br>59725-59744 |
| **Former Numbers:** | — | — |
| **Introduced:** | 1960 | 1960 |
| **Built by:** | BR Derby | BR Derby |
| **Engine Manufacturer:** | Leyland Albion | — |
| **Horsepower (total):** | 460 | — |
| **Weight of Car:** | 38.5 tonnes | 29.5 tonnes |
| **Length over Body:** | 19.50m | 19.42m |
| **Height of Car:** | 3.77m | 3.77m |
| **Width of Car:** | 2.81m | 2.81m |
| **Brake Type:** | Vacuum | Vacuum |
| **Maximum Speed:** | 70mph (113km/hr) | 70mph (113km/hr) |
| **Internal Layout:** | High density | High density |
| **Seating:** | 78 Second | 106 Second |
| **Region of Allocation:** | Midland | Midland |
| **Depots of Allocation:** | AN, ME | ME, TS |
| **Works responsible for overhauls:** | Derby | Derby |

* Declassified to 70 Second, except those allocated to ME

Below:
*The 'standard' Derby front end design was used when the fleet of Class 115 was constructed in 1960 for LMR operation. Recognition between this class and those previously shown should cause little problem, as these are High Density sets and have an access door by each seating bay. The DMBS type vehicle is illustrated, which accommodates 78 second class passengers.* Colin J. Marsden

TC
59664-59678
59719-59724
59745-59764
—
1960
BR Derby
—
—
30.5 tonnes
19.42m
3.77m
2.81m
Vacuum
70mph (113km/hr)
High density
40 Second, 30 First*
Midland
AN, ME, TS
Derby

Top:
*Class 115 stock usually operates in 4-car formations: DMBS-TC-TS-DMBS, providing accommodation for 302 second and 30 first class passengers. At the inner end of DMBS vehicles is a small guard's and luggage compartment capable of taking 1¼ tons of luggage. Underslung equipment is of the standard type, consisting of engines, transmissions, heating and battery boxes. A Class 115 set stops at Bicester on a Marylebone-Banbury working.* Colin J. Marsden

Above:
*To operate between the Class 115 DMBS cars there are two trailer types: Trailer Second — TS, and Trailer Composite — TC. The TS car is very similar to those operating in Class 116 units and recognition is best achieved by reference to the car number. However as a guide, the seat backs on Class 115s are usually taller. TS No 59740 stands at Marylebone and clearly shows its underframe items, consisting mainly of heating, brake, battery and lighting modules.* Colin J. Marsden

Top:
*The TC vehicles of Class 115 are quite easily recognised, as the first class area extends for five seating bays, whereas the other classes having TC vehicles in high density sets, only have four bays for first class occupation. There are two toilets positioned between the first and second class areas. Underframe equipment is the same as on TS cars. A number of TC vehicles allocated to AN and TS have been downgraded for all second class occupancy.* Colin J. Marsden

Above:
*In 1985 Class 115s are allocated to Marylebone, Allerton and Tyseley depots, and all are painted in standard blue/grey livery. A number of the Marylebone allocated power cars during the nearly 1980s were fitted with power sanding equipment to overcome adhesion problems on the London-Aylesbury route; this equipment consists of a bogie-mounted sand box, an air input pipe and a laying pipe on the leading end. A Class 115 set passes Northolt Park with No 51664 leading on the 10.08 Banbury-Marylebone of 26 June 1984.* Colin J. Marsden

Left:
*It is likely that the Class 115 vehicles will remain in service for at least the next five years, and some vehicles probably longer. However if Marylebone station is closed and services diverted to other London termini a revised policy may spell the end for the class. The 10.38 Marylebone-High Wycombe is seen near Northolt Park during the summer of 1984.* Colin J. Marsden

Above:
*The Liverpool allocated Class 115 units which are maintained at Allerton, usually operate in 3-car formations. A unit is seen here at Manchester Oxford Road with a Liverpool working. Note that the former headcode box has been blanked off by a steel plate.* Brian Morrison

# Class 116

| | |
|---|---|
| **Car Type:** | DMBS |
| **Car Numbers:** | 51128-51140<br>53050-53091<br>53818-53870 |
| **Former Numbers:** | 50050-50091<br>50818-50870 |
| **Introduced:** | 1957 |
| **Built by:** | BR Derby |
| **Engine Manufacturer:** | Leyland |
| **Horsepower (total):** | 300 |
| **Weight of Car:** | 36.5 tonnes |
| **Length over Body:** | 19.5m |
| **Height of Car:** | 3.77m |
| **Width of Car:** | 2.81m |
| **Brake Type:** | Vacuum |
| **Maximum Speed:** | 70mph (113km/hr) |
| **Internal Layout:** | High density |
| **Seating:** | 65 Second |
| **Regions of Allocation:** | Eastern, Midland, Scottish, Western |
| **Depots of Allocation:** | AY, CF, SF, TS |
| **Works responsible for overhauls:** | Glasgow, Derby, Doncaster |

Above:
*A sizeable fleet of Derby High Density sets now classified as Class 116 was introduced from 1957 and examples are now allocated to all regions except the Southern. The DMBS cars are very similar to the Class 115 DMBS fleet but are recognisable by having a larger brake van and are not fitted with a roof-mounted headcode box. DMBS No 53852 is illustrated.* Colin J. Marsden

| DMS | TS |
|---|---|
| 51141-51153 | 59030-59041 |
| 53092-53133 | 59326-59375 |
| 53871-53923 | 59438-59448 |
| 50092-50133 | — |
| 50871-50923 | — |
| 1957 | 1957 |
| BR Derby | BR Derby |
| Leyland | — |
| 300 | — |
| 36.5 tonnes | 29.5 tonnes |
| 19.5m | 19.42m |
| 3.77m | 3.77m |
| 2.81m | 2.81m |
| Vacuum | Vacuum |
| 70mph (113km/hr) | 70mph (113km/hr) |
| High density | High density |
| 95 Second | 100 Second |
| Eastern, Midland, Scottish, Western | Eastern, Midland, Scottish, Western |
| AY, CF, SF, TS | AY, CF, ED, SF, TS |
| Glasgow, Derby, Doncaster | Glasgow, Derby, Doncaster |

Above:
*To operate at the opposite ends of formations to DMBS cars, a fleet of DMS vehicles was constructed. These cars have nine seating bays, each with a side door; the accommodation is for 103 passengers in the 3+2 mode. A Class 116 set led by a DMS arrives at Four Oaks during 1984.* Colin J. Marsden

Top:
*The Class 116 TS vehicles can accommodate 100 passengers in 10 seating bays, again each with its own side door. Underframe equipment is sparse, with lighting, battery, brake and coach heating equipment being the main items. Note the bogie steps and bodyside grab handle at the far end enabling staff to climb aboard from ground level. Some vehicles of this type have had within-unit corridor connections fitted, thus reducing the seating by 10 on TS cars. No 59334 stands at Barnt Green.*
Colin J. Marsden

Above:
*Class 116 vehicles are allocated to AY, CF, ED, SF and TS depots, and usually operate in 3-car formations. Livery applied is currently blue/grey, but those allocated to ScR are likely to be repainted in Strathclyde PTE colours. A Class 116 set, formed with a Class 101 TS, passes Whitacre Junction on 15 July 1984 with an empty stock train.*
John Tuffs

Top right:
*Following the withdrawal of Class 127 stock from the St Pancras suburban lines a number of trailer vehicles were re-allocated to Tyseley for use with Class 116 stock. Here former Class 127 TS No 59597 is formed in a Class 116 set. These non-standard formations are recognisable by the TS having a toilet.* Colin J. Marsden

Above:
*Class 116 set in original as built condition in 1957, painted in green livery with yellow numbering and the distinctive yellow chevron on the front end. Note that when built these sets had additional front lamps above the destination indicator, and in the centre just above the buffer beam, both of which have now been removed.*
Author's Collection

Below:
*Underframe equipment on Class 116 DMBS/DMS vehicle. The coach heating unit can be seen on the left; in the middle the main electrical control box is located, and on the right the 150hp Leyland power unit, with exhaust pipe below.* Colin J. Marsden

# Class 117

| Car Type: | DMBS | DMS |
|---|---|---|
| Car Numbers: | 51332-51373 | 51374-51415 |
| Former Numbers: | — | — |
| Introduced: | 1959 | 1959 |
| Built by: | Pressed Steel | Pressed Steel |
| Engine Manufacturer: | Leyland | Leyland |
| Horsepower (total): | 300 | 300 |
| Weight of Car: | 36.5 tonnes | 36.5 tonnes |
| Length over Body: | 19.5m | 19.46m |
| Height of Car: | 3.87m | 3.87m |
| Width of Car: | 2.81m | 2.81m |
| Brake Type: | Vacuum | Vacuum |
| Maximum Speed: | 70mph (113km/hr) | 70mph (113km/hr) |
| Internal Layout: | High density | High density |
| Seating: | 65 Second | 89 Second |
| Region of Allocation: | Western | Western |
| Depots of Allocation: | BR, RG | BR, RG |
| Works responsible for overhauls: | Swindon | Swindon |

Below:
*This fleet of 122 coaches forming Class 117 was built by Pressed Steel and closely resembles the Derby units described in previous sections, but members are recognisable from the previously described Class 116 units by the fitting of a four-position route indicator box on the cab roof line (now painted out on most units). The unit illustrated here has its DMBS leading, which accommodates 65 passengers. Set B425 with car No 51363 leading, approaches Clink Road junction on a Westbury-Weymouth working on 31 August 1984.* Colin J. Marsden

TC
59484-59522
—
1959
Pressed Steel
—
—
30.5 tonnes
19.5m
3.87m
2.81m
Vacuum
70mph (113km/hr)
High density
48 Second, 22 First
Western
BR, RG
Swindon

Top:
*All Class 117 units are allocated to WR and operate from Bristol and Reading depots, mainly on suburban diagrams. All cars are painted in blue/grey livery and usually remain in 'set' formations for extended periods; they can be identified by their three-digit location-prefixed numbers. A DMS type vehicle leads in this view at Reading.* Colin J. Marsden

Above:
*The middle car of the Class 117 sets is a TC, laid out in the high density style, accommodating 48 second and 22 first class passengers, with two toilets towards the middle of the vehicle. This out of formation picture clearly shows the end layout with cropped buffers. Underframe equipment is of the conventional layout. Note the effluent drop pipe under the toilet.* Colin J. Marsden

# Class 118

| Car Type: | DMBS | DMS |
|---|---|---|
| Car Numbers: | 51302-51316 | 51317-51331 |
| Former Numbers: | — | — |
| Introduced: | 1960 | 1960 |
| Built by: | BRCW | BRCW |
| Engine Manufacturer: | Leyland | Leyland |
| Horsepower (total): | 300 | 300 |
| Weight of Car: | 36.5 tonnes | 36.5 tonnes |
| Length over Body: | 19.5m | 19.5m |
| Height of Car: | 2.87m | 2.87m |
| Width of Car: | 2.81m | 2.81m |
| Brake Type: | Vacuum | Vacuum |
| Maximum Speed: | 70mph (113km/hr) | 70mph (113km/hr) |
| Internal Layout: | High density | High density |
| Seating: | 65 Second | 89 Second |
| Region of Allocation: | Western | Western |
| Depots of Allocation: | BR, LA | BR, LA |
| Works responsible for overhauls: | Swindon | Swindon |

TC
59469-59483
—
1960
BRCW
—
—
30.5 tonnes
19.46m
2.87m
2.81m
Vacuum
70mph (113km/hr)
High density
48 Second, 22 First*
Western
BR, LA
Swindon

* All now declassified and seat 70 Second

Left:
*Another class of unit that closely follows the standard Derby design is this batch of 15 3-car units making up Class 118, all are allocated to the Western Region at BR and LA. Recognition between these and the Class 117 is very difficult, with only minor differences between them, one that might assist is the slightly shaped top to the route indicator box on these Class 118 units compared to the flat top on the Class 117s. P461 formed with two all-blue driving cars flanking a blue/grey trailer, stands at Exeter.* Colin J. Marsden

Above:
*The Class 118 DMS cars are again virtually identical to the corresponding Class 117 vehicles, recognition being best achieved by car numbers. An interesting feature within Class 118 is that at least three different buffer designs exist, noticeable if the three illustrations in this section are compared. Set No P463 arrives at Paignton with its DMS leading.* Colin J. Marsden

Right:
*The centre vehicle of Class 118 sets is now a TS, but when introduced the cars were laid out for first and second class occupation and were thus TCs. This illustration shows the front end and roof layout of set No P473 standing in the bay at Truro on a Falmouth shuttle service.* Colin J. Marsden

# Class 119

| Car Type: | DMBC | DMS |
|---|---|---|
| Car Numbers: | 51052-51079 | 51080-51107 |
| Former Numbers: | — | — |
| Introduced: | 1958 | 1958 |
| Built by: | Gloucester RCW | Gloucester RCW |
| Engine Manufacturer: | Leyland | Leyland |
| Horsepower (total): | 300 | 300 |
| Weight of Car: | 37.5 tonnes | 38.5 tonnes |
| Length over Body: | 19.66m | 19.66m |
| Height of Car: | 3.87m | 3.87m |
| Width of Car: | 2.81m | 2.81m |
| Brake Type: | Vacuum | Vacuum |
| Maximum Speed: | 70mph (113km/hr) | 70mph (113km/hr) |
| Internal Layout: | Cross-Country | Cross-Country |
| Seating: | 16 Second, 18 First | 68 Second |
| Region of Allocation: | Western | Western |
| Depots of Allocation: | BR, RG | BR, RG |
| Works responsible for overhauls: | Swindon | Swindon |

Above:
*The third class to be of similar design to the Derby-built standards is this fleet of Gloucester Railway Carriage & Wagon Cross-Country units. There are 25 3-car sets currently in traffic. The DMBC vehicles of this fleet have three bays for first class accommodation behind the driving cab, which is followed by a transverse walkway and then two second class bays. The remaining third of the coach contains the guard's van and a passenger luggage stowage area; this being provided for the extra amounts of luggage carried on the Reading-Gatwick line, where the sets are usually used. DMBC No 51065 is illustrated.* Colin J. Marsden

TS
59413-59437
—
1958
Gloucester RCW
—
—
31.5 tonnes
19.66m
3.87m
2.81m
Vacuum
70mph (113km/hr)
Cross-Country
60 Second
Western
BR, RG
Swindon

Above:
*The DMS cars of this class are similar to the corresponding type within Class 107 but of course do not have four-position route indicator box and are long framed cars. Accommodation is for 68 second class passengers in the 2+2 mode, with a toilet at the inner end. A 3-car Class 119 formation approaches Guildford with a Gatwick-Reading working with its DMS car leading.* Colin J. Marsden

Below:
*The TS type vehicles that operate within Class 119 are former Trailer Second Buffets, which now have the buffet facility removed and a passenger luggage stowage area provided in its place. The total seating is for 60 passengers. The two sides of these vehicles differ, with on one side one window position being plated over (this was behind the original buffet). No 59422 is shown from the former buffet end. Note the two empty equipment cases on the underframe, where originally the gas bottles for cooking were housed.* Colin J. Marsden

# Class 120

| | | |
|---|---|---|
| **Car Type:** | DMS | DMBC |
| **Car Numbers:** | 51582-51590<br>51788-51794<br>53647-53695 | 51573-51581<br>51781-51782<br>53696-53744 |
| **Former Numbers:** | 50647-50695 | 50696-50744 |
| **Introduced:** | 1957-69 | 1957-60 |
| **Built by:** | BR Swindon | BR Swindon |
| **Engine Manufacturer:** | AEC | AEC |
| **Horsepower (total):** | 300 | 300 |
| **Weight of Car:** | 37.6 tonnes | 36.5 tonnes |
| **Length over Body:** | 19.66m | 19.66m |
| **Height of Car:** | 3.77m | 3.77m |
| **Width of Car:** | 2.81m | 2.81m |
| **Brake Type:** | Vacuum | Vacuum |
| **Maximum Speed:** | 70mph (113km/hr) | 70mph (113km/hr) |
| **Internal Layout:** | Cross-Country | Cross-Country |
| **Seating:** | 68 Second | 16 Second, 18 First |
| **Regions of Allocation:** | Western, Midland | Western, Midland |
| **Depots of Allocation:** | CF, DY, NH | CF, CH, DY, NH |
| **Works responsible for overhauls:** | None scheduled | None scheduled |

| DMBF | TS |
|---|---|
| 51783-51787 | 59256-59301 |
| — | 59580-59588* |
| — | 59679-59685 |
| — | — |
| 1957-60 | 1957-60 |
| BR Swindon | BR Swindon |
| AEC | — |
| 300 | — |
| 37.6 tonnes | 31.5 tonnes |
| 19.66m | 19.66m |
| 3.77m | 3.77m |
| 2.81m | 2.81m |
| Vacuum | Vacuum |
| 70mph (113km/hr) | 70mph (113km/hr) |
| Cross-Country | Cross-Country |
| 18 First | 60 (68*) Second |
| Midland | Western, Midland |
| NH | CF, DY, NH, RG |
| None scheduled | None scheduled |

Below:
*The third design of Class 120 Motor Coach is the Driving Motor Brake First (DMBF). On these four cars, the three bays behind the driving cab are again for 18 first class passengers in the 2+1 style; this is followed by a transverse walkway. The remaining half coach is not for public use, containing guard's accommodation, security cage and luggage stowage area. All cars of this type are allocated to NH depot. The car illustrated, No 51785, is carrying a headlight between the two front windows as used on the Central Wales line.* Tom Clift

Above left:
*Internally similar to the Class 119s, this sizeable fleet of Class 120 Cross-Countries was the BR version. There are no fewer than three different Driving Motor types within the class. Firstly there is the Driving Motor Second (DMS), these seat 64 passengers in seven bays and have a toilet at the inner end, with two passenger doors provided on either side of the vehicle. DMS No 50648 is seen approaching Derby.* Colin J. Marsden

Left:
*The second Power Car type is the Driving Motor Brake Composite (DMBC). On these there is first class seating for 18 passengers in three bays of 2+1, directly behind the driving cab. This is followed by a transverse walkway and then two bays of second class seating; the inner third of the vehicle taken up by a guard's office and luggage space. A DMBC leads in this night study of a set at Derby.* Colin J. Marsden

Below:
*To operate between the various Class 120 driving cars are a number of TS vehicles, two different designs are in service. Nos 59256-301, 679-685 were built as Trailer Seconds with a miniature buffet at one end, which is now disused, seating 60 second class passengers. Cars Nos 59580-88 were purpose-built Trailer Seconds and accommodate 68 passengers. TS No 59301 is shown, a former miniature buffet car. This car is unusual as it is mounted on B4 bogies, fitted in an attempt to improve the riding quality.*
Colin J. Marsden

Bottom:
*Class 120 sets are painted in blue/grey livery and are presently allocated to CF, CH, DY, NH and RG depots, operating mainly on their intended cross-country services. A 3-car Class 120 formed DMS, TS (ex-miniature buffet), DMBC, leads a 3-car Class 101 at Lakenheath with the 11.17 Birmingham-Yarmouth (not Norwich as on blind) of 11 July 1981.* John C. Baker

Below:
*Some minor detail differences exist within the class; when built all Driving cars had four front marker lights, one at centre top and three above buffer beam height. Today only two are used (one above each buffer), the other two being progressively removed. A set formed DMS, TS (ex-buffet), DMBC approaches Derby on a Birmingham-Nottingham service.* Colin J. Marsden

Bottom:
*Like a number of DMU types, misformations do occur on an ever increasing scale and, in the case of Class 120s, this usually involves the use of Class 101 TS vehicles in place of life-expired Class 120 cars. A 3-car set formed of Class 120 DMBC, Class 101 TS, and Class 120 DMB passes Wetmore Sidings near Burton on Trent with a Birmingham-Lincoln train, a route where they are commonly to be found.*
Colin J. Marsden

## Class 121

| | | |
|---|---|---|
| **Car Type:** | DMBS | DTS |
| **Car Numbers:** | 55020-55034 | 54280-54289 |
| **Former Numbers:** | — | 56280-56289 |
| **Introduced:** | 1960 | 1960 |
| **Built by:** | Pressed Steel | Pressed Steel |
| **Engine Manufacturer:** | Leyland | — |
| **Horsepower (total):** | 300 | — |
| **Weight of Car:** | 38 tonnes | 30 tonnes |
| **Length over Body:** | 19.66m | 19.51m |
| **Height of Car:** | 3.77m | 3.77m |
| **Width of Car:** | 2.81m | 2.81m |
| **Brake Type:** | Vacuum | Vacuum |
| **Maximum Speed:** | 70mph (113km/hr) | 70mph (113km/hr) |
| **Internal Layout:** | High density | High density |
| **Seating:** | 65 Second | 91 Second |
| **Region of Allocation:** | Western | Western |
| **Depots of Allocation:** | BR, CF, LA, RG | RG |
| **Works responsible for overhauls:** | Swindon | Swindon |

Below:
*This fleet of 23 vehicles making up Class 121 is rather unusual as 15 of them are single power cars equipped with a driving position at each end, whilst the remainder are Driving Trailer Seconds (DTS) equipped with a cab at one end only. All are high density vehicles. DMBS No 55032, with brake van end nearest the camera, departs from Severn Tunnel Junction on a local to Cardiff.* Colin J. Marsden

Top right:
*The 10 DTS cars are virtually the same as the Class 117 DMS stock except for the omission of power equipment. These trailer cars were designed for operation with their powered brothers, but in practice operate with a variety of power cars and sets. In this illustration car No 54289 provides extra accommodation on the front of a Class 117 set passing West Ealing. DTS cars accommodate 91 passengers.* Colin J. Marsden

Centre right:
*Here a Class 121 twin, formed DTS, DMBS, is attached to the front end of a 3-car Class 117 set on a Bourne End-Paddington peak hour service. Class 121 DMBS cars are allocated to BR, CF, LA and RG, while the DTS vehicles are confined to the London division at RG. All vehicles are painted in blue/grey livery and all, except Nos 55032/3 are refurbished. In 1985 car No 55020 was painted in mock GWR chocolate & cream livery.*
Colin J. Marsden

Right:
*Occasionally, if the WR is short of a DMBS or DMS for a Class 117, a Class 121 DMBS may be substituted. This in no way affects the traction performance of the set but, of course, precludes the guard from having access throughout the train as no end corridor connections are provided on Class 121 stock. DMBS No 55027 provides the leading power car for a Class 117 set at Appleford en route for Oxford on 17 March 1984.* John C. Baker

# Class 122

**Car Type:** DMBS
**Car Numbers:** 55000-55012
**Former Numbers:** —
**Introduced:** 1958
**Built by:** Gloucester RCW
**Engine Manufacturer:** AEC
**Horsepower (total):** 300
**Weight of Car:** 36.5 tonnes
**Length over Body:** 19.66m
**Height of Car:** 3.77m
**Width of Car:** 2.81m
**Brake Type:** Vacuum
**Maximum Speed:** 70mph (113km/hr)
**Internal Layout:** High density
**Seating:** 65 Second
**Region of Allocation:** Midland
**Depot of Allocation:** TS
**Works responsible for overhauls:** Doncaster

Right:
*View showing 'non-exhaust' end of Class 122. Each vehicle is fitted with two AEC220 150hp engines, weighs 36.5 tonnes and can accommodate 65 second class passengers in the high density style. Car No 55005 leaves Guide Bridge on 11 July 1984 with the 12.15 Stockport-Stalybridge service.* John Tuffs

Below right:
*The present fleet of Class 122 numbers nine; all are allocated to TS depot and are mainly used in the West Midlands PTE area. With brake van nearest the camera No 55003 takes the line to Stratford-upon-Avon at Hatton, while forming the 11.05 Leamington Spa-Stratford-upon-Avon on 23 August 1984.* John Tuffs

Above:
*This fleet of Gloucester RCW-built single cars emerged prior to the previously described Class 121s. External appearance is similar and recognition of the two types is confined to the front ends, on these Class 122s the exhaust stacks are of a different design, and a roof mounted destination indicator is supplied, unlike the later-built units that were provided with a four-position route indicator. DMBS No 55012 is illustrated at Stourbridge Town on a Stourbridge Junction shuttle.* Colin J. Marsden

# Class 127

**Car Type:** TS
**Car Numbers:** 59589-59648
**Former Numbers:** —
**Introduced:** 1959
**Built by:** BR Derby
**Engine Manufacturer:** —
**Horsepower (total):** —
**Weight of Car:** 30 tonnes
**Length over Body:** 19.41m
**Height of Car:** 3.77m
**Width of Car:** 2.81m
**Brake Type:** Vacuum
**Maximum Speed:** 70mph (113km/hr)
**Internal Layout:** High density
**Seating:** 90 or 106 Second*
**Region of Allocation:** Midland
**Depot of Allocation:** TS
**Works responsible for overhauls:** N/A

* Cars 59589-617 have two toilets and seat 90 Second. Cars 59619-648 seat 106 Second.

Above:
*After the demise of the Class 127 diesel-hydraulic sets from the St Pancras-Bedford route most driving cars were scrapped. However it was decided that the two types of Trailer vehicle TS and TS with toilet, were suitable for further use. A total of 44 cars were re-allocated to TS for use with Class 116 sets. No 59607, a TS with toilet (incorrectly coded TC on the coach end) forms the middle vehicle of a Class 116 set.*
Colin J. Marsden

# Class 127 (Parcels)

| | | |
|---|---|---|
| **Car Type:** | DMNV | DMPV |
| **Car Numbers:** | 55970-55979 | 55980-55989 |
| **Introduced:** | Rebuilt 1985 | Rebuilt 1985 |
| **Built by:** | BR Derby | BR Derby |
| **Engine Manufacturer:** | Rolls-Royce | Rolls-Royce |
| **Horsepower (total):** | 476 | 476 |
| **Weight of Car:** | — | — |
| **Length over Body:** | 19.5m | 19.5m |
| **Height of Car:** | 3.77m | 3.77m |
| **Width of Car:** | 2.81m | 2.81m |
| **Brake Type:** | Vacuum | Vacuum |
| **Maximum Speed:** | 70mph (113km/hr) | 70mph (113km/hr) |
| **Internal Layout:** | Parcels | Parcels |
| **Seating:** | None | None |
| **Region of Allocation:** | Midland | Midland |
| **Depots of Allocation:** | LO | LO |
| **Works responsible for overhauls:** | N/A | N/A |

Left:
*When it was decided to retain the Class 127 Trailers, a number were refurbished, and others were fitted with end gangways, thus reducing the accommodation by four seats. Not looking out of place a mixed Class 116/127/116 set approaches Redditch with a train from Four Oaks. All Class 127 trailer vehicles are now painted in blue/grey livery.*
Colin J. Marsden

Above:
*In mid-1985 a fleet of 10 2-car Motor Parcels sets, formed of former Class 127 DMBS vehicles coupled back to back, entered service in the Manchester area being allocated to Longsight depot. The vehicles have had all internal fittings removed, with newspaper sorting tables being added in some cases. Alterations have also been effected to the doors, and at least one set has acquired roller shutter style doors. Car No 55983 is illustrated at LO depot; livery applied is Rail Blue.* David Nicholas

# Class 128

**Car Type:** DMLV
**Car Numbers:** 55991-55995
**Former Numbers:** —
**Introduced:** 1959
**Built by:** Gloucester RCW
**Engine Manufacturer:** Leyland Albion
**Horsepower (total):** 460
**Weight of Car:** 40-41 tonnes
**Length over Body:** 19.65m
**Height of Car:** 3.87m
**Width of Car:** 2.81m
**Brake Type:** Vacuum
**Maximum Speed:** 70mph (113km/hr)
**Internal Layout:** Parcels
**Region of Allocation:** Midland, Western
**Depots of Allocation:** TS, RG
**Works responsible for overhauls:** None scheduled

Below:
*The Midland and Western Regions operate this fleet of single-car parcels vans known as DMLVs and classified as 128. All are equipped with a driving position at each end, and three double sized access doors for mail and goods on each side. All technical equipment is underfloor-mounted, and cars conform to the blue square coupling system. Illustrated here DMLV No 55991 approaches Acton while en route from Reading to Paddington during 1984.* Colin J. Marsden

Top right:
*Although now withdrawn, the first two cars, numerically Nos 55989/90 were rebuilt in the 1970s and had their gangway connections removed. This plate of car No 55989 at Manchester Victoria clearly shows the rather cluttered front end layout. Buffing and draw-gear is of the standard type.* Colin J. Marsden

Bottom right:
*The present fleet of five DMLVs is allocated thus: two to Reading, and three to Tyseley. The cars usually operate timetabled parcel services, either singly or in multiple with another DMMU, or hauling vacuum-braked van stock. WR allocated No 55991 in multiple with a Class 121, passes West Ealing with a Paddington-Reading parcels service.* Colin J. Marsden

# Class 140

**Unit Number:** 140.001
**Former Number:** —
**Introduced:** 1981
**Built by:** BR Derby
**Area of Use:** Plymouth local area*
**Weight of Unit:** 47 tonnes
**Length of Each Coach:** 16.02m
**Height:** 3.88m
**Width:** 2.46m
**Brake Type:** Electro-pneumatic
**Engine Type:** 2×Leyland TL11
**Horsepower:** 410
**Maximum Speed:** 75mph (121km/hr)
**Coupling Type:** Tightlock
**Coupling restriction:** Within type
**Formation & Seating:**
DMS 55500: 52 Second
DMS(L) 55501: 50 Second
**Depot of Allocation:** LA
**Works responsible for overhauls:**
Derby Technical Centre

* Or as required by Derby CM&EE Department for development and testing work.

Left:
*The Class 140 prototype visited a number of locations throughout the country for evaluation and training purposes. The set was used for passenger operation in a number of areas and the experience gained was developed into the production Class 141 sets. This view shows the very cluttered 'garden shed' type front end. Coupling provided by a 'Tightlock' coupler and air and control cables mounted either side of the end emergency door.* Colin J. Marsden

Bottom left:
*In 1981 the Railway Technical Centre, Derby, built, in collaboration with Leyland, a prototype 2-car unit; each coach was formed of Leyland 'National' bus body components mounted on a specially fabricated two-axle underframe. A single folding door was provided on one side of each coach, with two on the other side. Driving Motor Second with lavatory No 55501 stands at Cambridge soon after introduction in July 1981.* Keith Grafton

Below:
*The two Class 140 cars accommodate 94 seated passengers and there is sufficient room for about another 160 standing. Each car is fitted with a Leyland TL11 (205hp) engine, which drives the two pairs of wheels on that vehicle. At the time of writing the set is allocated to Laira and being used for depot staff and driver training in preparation for Class 142 sets being allocated to the West of England. Driving Motor Second No 55500 is illustrated.* Keith Grafton

# Class 141

**Unit Numbers:** 141.001-141.020*
**Former Numbers:** —
**Introduced:** 1983-84
**Built by:** Leyland/BREL Derby
**Area of Use:** South Yorkshire area
**Weight of Unit:** 52.5 tonnes
**Length of Each Coach:** 15.45m
**Height:** 3.88m
**Width:** 2.46m
**Brake Type:** Electro-pneumatic
**Engine Type:** 2×Leyland TL11
**Horsepower:** 410
**Maximum Speed:** 75mph (121km/hr)
**Coupling Type:** Tightlock
**Coupling restriction:** Within type and Class 142
**Formation & Seating:**
DMS 55502-55521: 50 Second
DMS(L) 55522-55541: 44 Second
**Depot of Allocation:** NL
**Works Responsible for Overhauls:** Derby

* Unit Numbers not carried.

**Note:**
The couplings of the Class 141 units are being modified to make them compatible with Class 142 and similar units.

Below:
*Following the successful design and testing of the BR/Leyland Class 140, a fleet of production Class 141 units was ordered in 1982, emerging towards the end of 1983, each unit being formed of two vehicles: a Driving Motor Second and a Driving Motor Second with lavatory. DMS(L) No 55530 leads in this picture at York while on a Leeds working.* Colin J. Marsden

Above:
*The recognition between the DMS and the DMS(L) is best achieved by looking for the frosted window adjacent to the toilet compartment in the DMS(L). Passenger access is by standard 'Leyland bus' folding doors on both sides of each coach, the driver having separate access to/from the cab by an inward opening hinged door. DMS(L) No 55529 is photographed with the toilet end nearest to the camera.* Colin J. Marsden

Above:
*Class 141 DMS from cab end. Each Class 141 vehicle is mounted on a special 4-wheel chassis and powered by a TL11, 205hp engine. Accommodation in each vehicle is for second class passengers, 44 seats in the DMS(L) and 50 in the DMS. However at the design stage special attention was paid to ensure that sufficient room was provided for an equal number of standing passengers in each coach. DMS No 55509 is illustrated.*
Colin J. Marsden

# Class 142

**Unit Numbers:** 142.001-142.050
**Former Numbers:** —
**Introduced:** 1985-86
**Built by:** Leyland/BREL Derby
**Area of Use:** Manchester PTE, West of England
**Weight of Unit:** —
**Length of Each Coach:** —
**Height:** —
**Width:** —
**Brake Type:** Electro-pneumatic
**Engine Type:** 2×Leyland TL11
**Horsepower:** 410
**Maximum Speed:** 75mph (121km/hr)
**Coupling Type:** Tightlock
**Coupling restriction:** Within type and Class 141
**Formation & Seating:**
DMS 55542-55591
DMS(L) 55592-55641
**Depot of Allocation:** NH, LA
**Works Responsible for Overhauls:** Derby

Left:
*The Class 142 front end is far removed from that of the original Class 140 prototype and indeed far more pleasing to the eye than the Class 141. Again no buffers are provided and all forces are transmitted via a centre tightlock coupler which has an electrical connection box below. Adjacent to the centre coupler behind a mesh screen are the two-tone warning horns. On the nose end, under the three windows are two standard lamp clusters; housing headlight, marker lights and tail indicators.* John Tuffs

Bottom left:
*The first of 50 2-car wide-bodied 'railbus' sets emerged from BREL Derby in the summer of 1985 classified as 142. Similar to the Class 141 units, the bus body based passenger portion was fabricated by British Leyland at Workington and married to a 4-wheel chassis built at Derby. The DMS(L) of the first set is illustrated.* John Tuffs

Below:
*Passenger access to vehicles is by conventional folding-style bus-type doors under the overall control of the trainmen, but with local opening push puttons. One door is provided on the driver's side directly behind his position, and two doors on the non-driving side. Unit No 142.015 in Western Region brown and cream livery stands outside Laira depot. DMSL No 55606 is nearest the camera.* Colin J. Marsden

# Class 143

**Unit Numbers:** 143.001-143.025
**Former Numbers:** —
**Introduced:** 1985-86
**Built by:** W. Alexander & Sons/ A.Barclay
**Area of Use:** North East suburban
**Weight of Unit:** —
**Length of Each Coach:** —
**Height:** —
**Width:** —
**Brake Type:** Electro-pneumatic
**Engine Type:** —
**Horsepower:** —
**Maximum Speed:** 75mph (121km/hr)
**Coupling Type:** Tightlock
**Coupling Restriction:** Within type
**Formation & Seating:**

| | |
|---|---|
| DMS | 55642-55666 |
| DMS(L) | 55667-55691 |

**Depot of Allocation:** HT
**Works Responsible for Overhauls:** —

Below:
*The summer of 1985 saw the commencement of deliveries of Class 143 twin railbuses built by W. Alexander/ A. Barclay for use in the Tyneside area. The sets are very similar to the Class 142 type, each coach having a folding door on the driving side, and two on the non-driving side. Set No 143.001 is illustrated at Matlock in October 1985 during trial running.*
John Tuffs

Right:
*Class 143 front end. The main colour for the cab ends is yellow with black relief round the three frontal windows. Two lamp clusters are located towards the lower front, each containing a side, head and tail light. A standard tightlock coupler with electrical connection box is provided in the centre, whilst a battery box and horns are situated behind the underfront skirt.* John Tuffs

Below:
*The Class 143 vehicles are mounted on a four-wheel chassis with a fixed coupling between vehicles. This view of the between vehicle coupling arrangement shows the inner end folding door, exhaust stack, toilet water filling point and battery boxes. All Class 143 units are painted in provincial sector colours.* John Tuffs

# Class 150

**Unit Numbers:** 150.001-150.002
**Former Numbers:** —
**Introduced:** 1984
**Built by:** BREL York
**Area of Use:** LMR*
**Weight of Unit:** 102.00 tonnes
**Length of Each Coach:** 19.93m
**Height:** 3.77m
**Width:** 2.82m
**Brake Type:** Electro-pneumatic
**Engine Type:**
150.001: 3×Cummins NT855RS
150.002: 3×Rolls-Royce 'Eagle'
**Horsepower:**
150.001: 855
150.002: 840
**Maximum Speed:** 75mph (121km/hr)
**Coupling Type:** Tightlock
**Coupling restriction:** Within type and Class 142, 151

**Formation & Seating:**

| | |
|---|---|
| DMS | 55200-1: 76 Second |
| MS | 55400: 150.001: 87 Second |
| | 55401: 150.002: 84 Second |
| DMS | 55300-1: 79 Second |

**Depot of Allocation:** DY
**Works Responsible for Overhauls:** York

* Used for test operation at a number of locations.

**Note**
As this book went to press the first Class 150 'production' two-car sets emerged from BREL York works. The sets are formed of two Driving Motor Seconds (DMS), and are expected to replace Class 120 sets on the Midland Region.

Below:
*During 1984 two prototype 3-car Class 150 sets were introduced, being built by York BREL. The units incorporated a body design based on the Class 317/455 electric sets. A break from previous diesel unit practice is that each car is powered, unit No 150.001 has Cummins 285hp power units while set No 150.002 has Rolls-Royce 'Eagle' 280hp prime movers. Set No 150.001, showing its distinctive front end styling, stands at Matlock in early 1985.* Colin J. Marsden

Right:
*The two driving cars classified DMS are slightly different; one seats 79 second class passengers while the other has a small toilet and seats only 76. Passenger access is by two double leaf sliding doors on each side which are passenger-operated but under the over-riding control of the guard. Main underframe equipment consists of engine, coolant, heating, battery and lighting modules.* Colin J. Marsden

Below:

*Between the two DMS vehicles is a Motor Second (MS) which in set No 150.001 seats 87, and in set No 150.002 accommodates 84. Again two pairs of double leaf doors are provided on each side and underframe equipment is basically the same as on Driving cars. The livery applied to both sets is a grey body with yellow and black front ends, there is a dark blue band at window height on the body sides with a narrow white and light blue strip below. At the present time the two units are allocated to Derby and normally operate on the Matlock branch. MS No 55401 from unit 150.002 is illustrated.*
Colin J. Marsden

# Class 151

**Unit Numbers:** 151.001-151.002
**Former Numbers:** —
**Introduced:** 1984
**Built by:** Metro-Cammell
**Area of Use:** LMR*
**Weight of Unit:** —
**Length of Each Coach:** —
**Height:** —
**Width:** —
**Brake Type:** Electro-pneumatic
**Engine Type:** 3×Cummins NT855RS
**Horsepower:** 855
**Maximum Speed:** 75mph (121km/hr)
**Coupling Type:** Tightlock
**Coupling restriction:** Within type, and Class 142, 150
**Formation & Seating:**

| | |
|---|---|
| DMS(L) | 55202-3: 80 Second |
| MS | 55402-3: 84 Second |
| DMS | 55302-3: 68 Second |

**Depot of Allocation:** DY
**Works Responsible for Overhauls:** York

* Used for test operation at a number of locations.

Below:
*As a design alternative to the BR Class 150, Metro-Cammell were contracted to build two 3-car sets, again each vehicle being powered. The first of the 3-car sets formed DMS, MS, DMS was delivered from Metro-Cammell in February 1985 and towards the end of the month commenced trial running on the Mickleover test track. In this view we see DMS No 55302 nearest the camera. This vehicle has accommodation for 68 second class passengers and has a chemical emission toilet. Passenger access is by two pairs of passenger-operated sliding doors.* John Tuffs

Above right:
*The intermediate vehicle of the Class 151 is a Motor Second (MS) with accommodation for 84. Access, as on the driving cars, is provided by two pairs of passenger-operated sliding doors which are under the overall supervision of the guard or, if single manned, the driver. Car No 55402 is shown.* John Tuffs

Below:
*DMS cars Nos 55202/3 provide seating for 80 passengers and look identical in appearance to DMS cars Nos 55402/3. The front end of these sets is most distinctive and should cause no problem with recognition. The exterior of coaches is also very distinctive with the roof-mounted ventilation module on each coach. Livery is silver with a blue and white body band. Set No 151.001 is seen near Etwell with a test train on the Mickleover test track on 27 February 1985 with car No 55202 leading.* John Tuffs

# Class 201

**Class Type:** 6S
**Proposed Unit Numbers:** 201101-201107
**Unit Numbers:** 1001-1007
**Introduced:** 1957
**Built by:** BR Eastleigh
**Area of Use:** London-Hastings line
**Weight of Unit:** 229 tonnes
**Length of Each Coach:** 17.67m
**Height:** 3.82m
**Width:** 2.74m
**Brake Type:** Auto air and electro-pneumatic
**Engine Type:** 2×EE6K
**Horsepower:** 1,000
**Maximum Speed:** 75mph (121km/hr)
**Coupling Type:** Buck-eye
**Coupling restriction:** Within DEMU type
**Formation & Seating:**

| | |
|---|---|
| DMBS | 22 Second |
| TS | 52 Second |
| TC | 36 First, 6 Second |
| TS | 52 Second |
| TS | 52 Second |
| DMBS | 22 Second |

**Depot of Allocation:** SE
**Works Responsible for Overhauls:** Eastleigh

Right:
*With the intention to eliminate steam traction from the London-Hastings line, a fleet of main line Diesel Electric Multiple-Units (DEMU) were authorised under the 1955 Modernisation Plan. Each set was to have a power car at each end flanking a number of Trailer vehicles. Two basic types of 'Hastings' unit were constructed; some sets were formed of 'long-framed' vehicles and others of 'short'. Cars can be identified by the window layout. 6S (6-car 'short-framed') set No 1002 passes Hither Green with a Charing Cross-Hastings service in October 1982.* Colin J. Marsden

Below:
*Class 201 (6S) Drawing.*

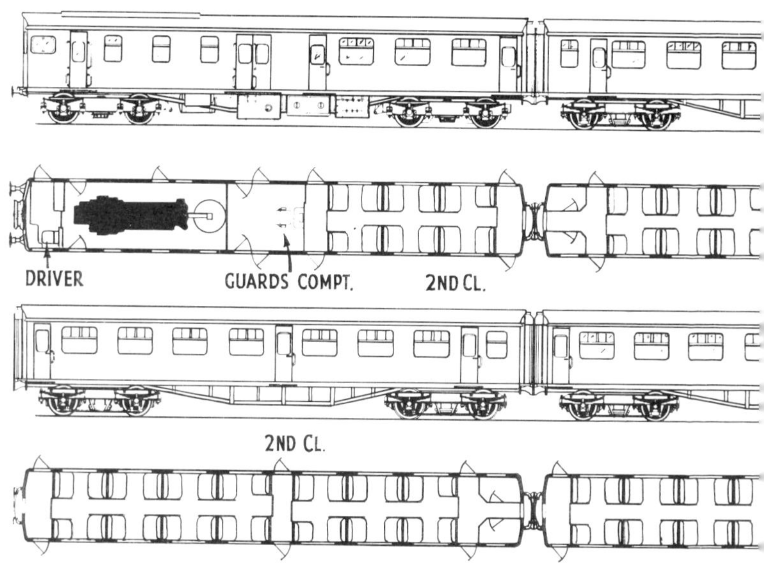

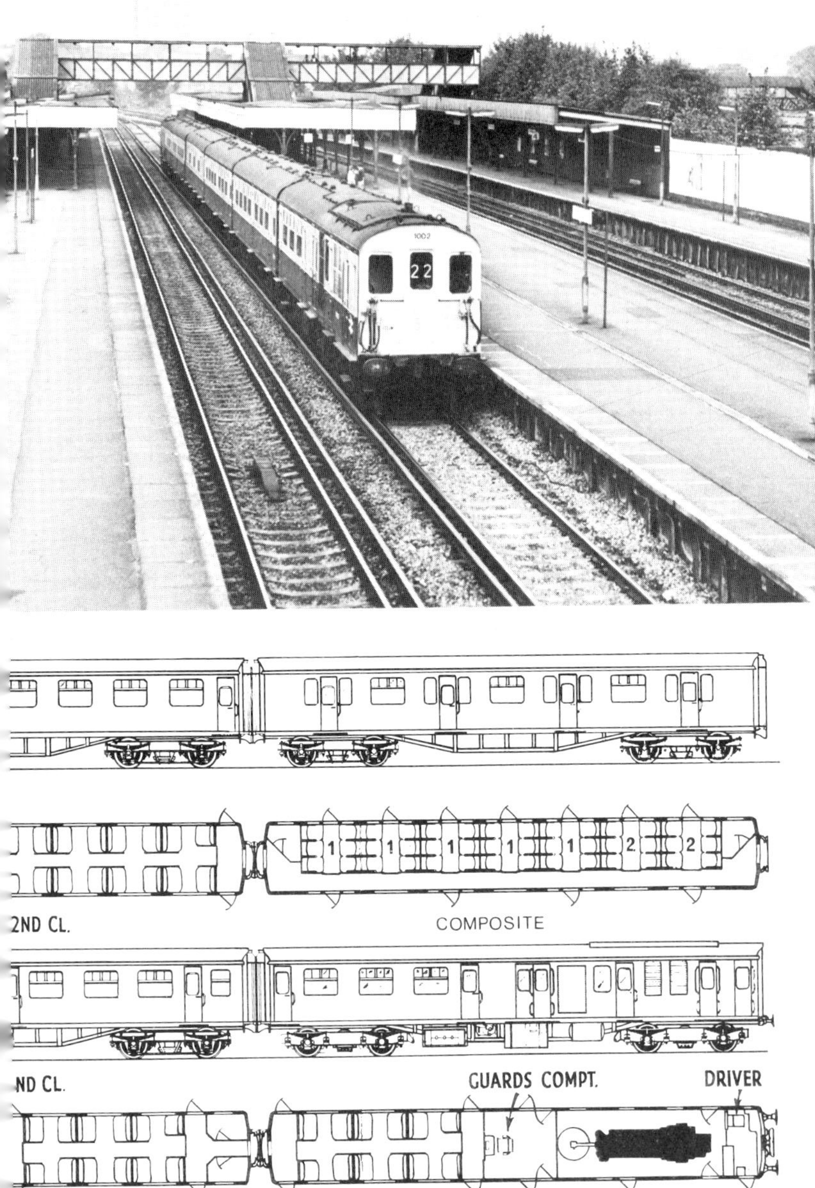
1002
22
1
1
1
1
1
2
2
2ND CL.
COMPOSITE
ND CL.
GUARDS COMPT.
DRIVER

Above:
*The Class 201 DMBS vehicles have a full width driving cab at the outer ends, with controls on the left side, to the rear is a transverse walkway, and behind is the engine and equipment room. On the body side adjacent to the power unit (on the driving side) are three glazed windows, while on the other side there are air louvres. To the rear of the engine compartment is the guard's brake van, a transverse walkway and three seating bays, total passenger accommodation being for 22 second class passengers. Two Class 201 DMBS vehicles unusually displaying a black nose triangle, flank the BRB High Speed Test Car.* Colin J. Marsden

Below:
*Between the two DMBS cars are four short-framed Trailers: three Trailer Seconds (TS) and one Trailer Composite (TC). The TS cars have two toilets at one end, followed by a full width walkway, three seating bays, a full width walkway, four seating bays and another transverse walkway. Seating is in the 2+2 mode. TS No 60519 is illustrated from unit No 1007.* Colin J. Marsden

Above:
*All Class 201 (6S) units are allocated to St Leonards depot near Hastings and are painted in blue/grey livery. The sets will remain in traffic until the electrification of the London-Hastings line is completed. 6S No 1004 incorrectly formed with a 6L TC, forms the 11.45 Charing Cross-Hastings on 10 August 1982, seen passing Tunbridge Wells Central goods yard.* Colin J. Marsden

Below:
*The present Trailer Composite (TC) vehicle was built as a Trailer First (TF) having seven six-seat compartments, a toilet at each end and a side corridor. However with the gradual decline in first class patronage it was decided to de-classify one compartment and thus provide accommodation for 36 first and six second class passengers. 6S No 1007 stands at St Leonards with a TC vehicle third from front.* Colin J. Marsden

# Class 202, 203*

**Class Type:** 6L, 5L*
**Proposed Unit Numbers:**
202201-202211, 203301-203304*
**Unit Numbers:** 1011-1032, 1034-1037*
**Introduced:** 1957-58
**Built by:** BR Eastleigh
**Area of Use:** London-Hastings line
**Weight of Unit:** 235 tonnes, 204.5 tonnes*
**Length of Each Coach:** 19.67m
**Height:** 3.82m
**Width:** 2.74m
**Brake Type:** Auto air and electro-pneumatic
**Engine Type:** 2×EE6K
**Horsepower:** 1,000
**Maximum Speed:** 75mph (121km/hr)
**Coupling Type:** Buck-eye
**Coupling restriction:** Within DEMU type
**Formation & Seating:**

| | |
|---|---|
| DMBS | 30 Second |
| TS | 60 Second |
| TC | 36 First, 12 Second |
| TS | 60 Second |
| TS | 60 Second† |
| DMBS | 30 Second |

**Depot of Allocation:** SE
**Works Responsible for Overhauls:** Eastleigh

* Formerly 6B units.
† Not in Class 203

Below:
*Although at a first glance members of Classes 202 and 203 look identical to those of Class 201, a number of differences do exist, aiding in their recognition. The main difference is that Classes 202 and 203 vehicles are built on long-frames, giving one extra seating bay in each vehicle. Class 202 No 1031 is seen here near Petts Wood early in 1982.* Colin J. Marsden

Right:
*Class 202 front end detail (applies to all SR DEMU stock):* ***1*** *Multiple unit control jumper cable,* ***2*** *Air brake pipe,* ***3*** *Main reservoir pipe (dual cock with air brake pipe,* ***4*** *Multiple unit control jumper receptacle,* ***5*** *Air warning horns,* ***6*** *Pullman rubbing plate,* ***7*** *Buck-eye coupling,* ***8*** *Buck-eye release chain.* Colin J. Marsden

Note: *Members of Class 203 (5L) are former 6B buffet car units, which now operate minus their buffet vehicles.*

5
5
1017
2
3
3
2
1
4
Class 202
6L
6
7
8

Below:
*Classes 202/3 DMBS: the layout of the cab, engine room and guard's area is identical to the Class 201, however passenger accommodation on these long-framed cars is for 30, set out in four bays. Underframe-mounted equipment consists of battery boxes, fuel tank, brake units and air reservoirs. Three cars of set No 1018 stand at Eastleigh works during 1979.* Colin J. Marsden

Bottom:
*Long Framed Trailer Second: if this and the illustration of the short-framed TS are compared, it will be observed that recognition is very easy between the two types. Seating in short-frame cars is provided in one three-bay and one four-bay saloon, whereas on long-framed cars two four-bay saloons exist. Again there are two toilets provided at one end. TS No 60525 is illustrated.* Colin J. Marsden

Below:
*Again when built the long-framed sets had one coach designated for first class occupation and classified Trailer First (TF). In common with SR policy from the late 1970s, first class capacity was reduced, and on long-framed TF vehicles two compartments at one end were declassified, thus reclassifying the car as a Trailer Composite (TC). 6L TC No 60709 is illustrated.* Colin J. Marsden

Bottom:
*There are presently five 5L sets and nine 6Ls in operation. Like the short-framed sets all are allocated to St Leonards depot and usually operate only on their intended London-Hastings route. A 5L plus 6S formation led by 5L No 1035, departs from Etchingham on 10 August 1982 with a Hastings-Charing Cross service.*
Colin J. Marsden

# Class 204

**Class Type:** 3T
**Proposed Unit Numbers:** 204401-204404
**Unit Numbers:** 1401-1404
**Introduced:** 1979-80 rebuilt from 205/206 stock
**Built by:** BR Eastleigh
**Area of Use:** Hampshire non-electrified routes
**Weight of Unit:** 118 tonnes
**Length of Each Coach:** DMBS, DTC: 19.51m, DTS (Middle): 19.50m
**Height:** 3.82m
**Width:** 2.82m
**Brake Type:** Auto air and electro-pneumatic
**Engine Type:** EE6K
**Horsepower:** 600
**Maximum Speed:** 75mph (121km/hr)
**Coupling Type:** Buck-eye
**Coupling Restriction:** Within DEMU type
**Formation & Seating:**

| | |
|---|---|
| DMBS | 52 Second |
| DTS | 102 Second |
| DTC | 13 First, 50 Second |

**Depot of Allocation:** EH
**Works Responsible for Overhauls:** Eastleigh

Below:
*These four units making up Class 204 or 3T were formed from 1979 by reforming various Class 205 and 206 2/3H and 3R units. 3T sets are formed DTC/TS/DMBS. The TS vehicle is somewhat unusual as it is a former DTC car downgraded and converted to TS requirements. Unit No 1403 approaches Northam Junction in this photograph taken during 1984 with the DMBS car leading.* Colin J. Marsden

Right:
*Dummy driving end of TS coach, showing that the now disused cab end remains in situ but is rendered inoperative, and that the yellow warning end has been painted out, roof air horns remain in place but the buffer heads have been removed. Two additional jumpers are also carried under the cab window nearest the camera, the TS cars accommodate 66 passengers in the high density 2+3 mode. Since this picture was taken all four units have been painted in blue/grey livery.* Colin J. Marsden

Below:
*The four Class 204 units are allocated to Eastleigh and can usually be found operating on Hampshire area diagrams. Set No 1404 was photographed at Fratton depot during 1982 reposing between duties on the Portsmouth-Southampton-Salisbury line.*
Colin J. Marsden

# Class 205

**Class Type:** 3H
**Proposed Unit Numbers:** 205501-205529
**Unit Numbers:** 1101-1133
**Introduced:** 1957-62
**Built by:** BR Eastleigh
**Area of Use:** SR non-electrified routes
**Weight of Unit:** 118 tonnes
**Length of Each Coach:** DMBS, DTC: 10.51m; TSO: 19.34m
**Height:** 3.82m
**Width:** 2.82m
**Brake Type:** Auto air and electro-pneumatic
**Engine Type:** EE6K
**Horsepower:** 600
**Maximum Speed:** 75mph (121km/hr)
**Coupling Type:** Buck-eye
**Coupling Restriction:** Within DEMU type
**Formation & Seating:**

| | |
|---|---|
| DMBS | 52 Second* |
| TSO | 104 Second |
| DTC | See Note 1 |

**Depots of Allocation:** EH, SE
**Works Responsible for Overhauls:** Eastleigh

* Some DMBS seat 42 Second.
**Note:** Most DTC cars seat 19 First and 50 Second, but some units seat 13 First and 50 Second+Luggage Compartment, while others seat 13 First and 62 Second.
Unit No 205509 is refurbished and seats:

| | |
|---|---|
| DMBS | 39 Second |
| TS | 98 Second |
| DTS | 76 Second |

Below:
*Classified by the SR as 'Hampshire' units are the 29 members of Class 205 (3H). These units are formed DTC, TS, DMBS. The DTC vehicles are laid out in one of three different ways. Units Nos 1101-1105/09/20/24-26 accommodate 13 first class and 50 second class passengers, having the compartment directly behind the driver designated for luggage. On unit Nos 1127-33 the seating is for 13 first and 50 second class passengers. The remainder of the fleet accommodates 19 first and 50 second class seating; unit No 1101 being illustrated.*
Colin J. Marsden

Above right:
*This view is also of a Class 205 from the DTC end, but shows unit No 1113 which has the first three compartments behind the cab set out for first class occupation. Towards the centre of the coach are two toilets. At the inner end of the coach five bays of second class seats are provided. Unit No 1113 departs from Winnersh with a Reading-Tonbridge train.* Colin J. Marsden

Below:
*The intermediate vehicle within the Class 205 sets is a TS accommodating 104 passengers basically in the 2+3 high density mode. 10 passenger doors are provided on each side, one by each seating bay. Underframe equipment is sparse on these cars with the main item being brake control units. TS No 60667 from unit No 1118 is illustrated.*
Colin J. Marsden

Above and below:
*Power cars for Class 205 sets are provided by a fleet of DMBS vehicles. These have a full width driving compartment at the outer end, together with a transverse walkway behind; this is followed by the engine compartment and guard's/luggage area. The remaining half coach contains seating bays. On vehicles in sets Nos 1101-1126, five bays are provided while sets Nos 1127-1133 have only four. The four-bay sets are a later build (1962) and are also recognisable from others as they have a smaller headcode indicator. The first view shows set No 1118 with five seating bays, whilst the following plate is of 1962 built No 1127 with four seating bays and smaller headcode box.*
Both: Colin J. Marsden

Above:
*Class 205 sets are allocated to SE (St Leonards) and EH (Eastleigh) depots and can be found operating on all three SR sections, reaching the London area on the Central Division Victoria-Uckfield/East Grinstead services, and selected Salisbury-Waterloo services on Saturdays. Set No 1124 with the DTC nearest the camera, pulls away from Northam Junction on a Salisbury-Portsmouth train.* Colin J. Marsden

Below:
*Unit No 1111 was selected for extensive refurbishment at Eastleigh Works during 1979 and reclassified as 3H(M) — 3-car Hampshire unit modified. During refurbishing work gangways were fitted between coaches, fluorescent lighting installed, other work carried out included the fitting of a public address system and the removal of first class accommodation. The unit is allocated to St Leonards shed and is usually used on the Ashford-Hastings route. The unit number was unusually applied above each cab window rather than in the centre. No 1111 was photographed here at Ashford with its DMBS nearest the camera.* Brian Morrison

# Class 207

**Class Type:** 3D
**Proposed Unit Numbers:** 207701-207719
**Unit Numbers:** 1301-1319
**Introduced:** 1962
**Built by:** BR Eastleigh
**Area of Use:** SR non-electrified routes
**Weight of Unit:** 121.00 tonnes
**Length of Each Coach:** DMBS, DTS: 19.58m, TC: 19.36m
**Height:** 3.82m
**Width:** 2.74m
**Brake Type:** Auto air and electro-pneumatic
**Engine Type:** EE6K
**Horsepower:** 600
**Maximum Speed:** 75mph (121km/hr)
**Coupling Type:** Buck-eye
**Coupling Restriction:** Within DEMU type
**Formation & Seating:**

| | |
|---|---|
| DMBS | 42 Second |
| TC | 24 First, 42 Second |
| DTS | 76 Second |

**Depot of Allocation:** SE
**Works Responsible for Overhauls:** Eastleigh

Below:
*The most modern of the SR DEMU fleet emerged from Eastleigh works during 1962 when a fleet of 19 3-car sets was built for the Oxted line. Classification given was 3D which was later changed under the BR numerical policy to Class 207. The front end layout of units is of a more pleasing outline being fabricated in steel-reinforced fibreglass with air pipes and control cables being recessed. All units are fitted with the smaller size route indicator box. Unit No 1315 stands at Hurst Green with an Uckfield train.* Colin J. Marsden

Above:
*At the opposite end to the DMBS is a Driving Trailer Second (DTS) providing accommodation for 76 passengers in a high density open layout. Underframe equipment is kept to a minimum, mainly consisting of brake control equipment. All Class 207 units are allocated to St Leonards depot and usually operate on the Central and South East sections. Set No 1319 leads a Class 205 at Norwood Junction while forming a London Bridge-East Grinstead/Uckfield service during May 1982.*
Colin J. Marsden

Above:
*Operating as a middle car in the Class 207 formations is a Trailer Composite (TC). These TC coaches are unique to the SR DEMU fleet, in that they have the first class accommodation and toilet sandwiched between two and three second class seating bays, providing 24 first and 42 second class seats. Set No 1313 departs from Hurst Green bound for Uckfield.* Colin J. Marsden

# Class 210

| | | | | |
|---|---|---|---|---|
| **Unit Numbers:** | 210.001 | | 210.002 | |
| **Former Numbers:** | — | | — | |
| **Introduced:** | 1981 | | 1981 | |
| **Built by:** | BR Derby | | BR Derby | |
| **Area of Use:** | WR Suburban | | WR Suburban | |
| **Weight of Unit:** | 148 tonnes | | 118 tonnes | |
| **Length of Unit:** | 80.72m | | 60.52m | |
| **Height:** | 3.75m | | 3.75m | |
| **Width:** | 2.82m | | 2.82m | |
| **Brake Type:** | Electro-pneumatic | | Electro-pneumatic | |
| **Engine Type:** | Paxman RP200L | | MTU12U396 | |
| **Horsepower:** | 1,125 | | 1,140 | |
| **Maximum Speed:** | 75mph (121km/hr) | | 75mph (121km/hr) | |
| **Coupling Type:** | Tightlock | | Tightlock | |
| **Coupling Restrictions:** | Within type | | Within type | |
| **Formation & Seating:** | DMBS | 28 Second | DMS | 45 Second |
| | TS | 84 Second | TS | 84 Second |
| | TC | 22 First | DTS | 74 Second |
| | | 46 Second | | |
| | DTS | 74 Second | | |
| **Depot of Allocation:** | RG | | RG | |
| **Works responsible for overhauls:** | Derby | | Derby | |

Below:
*Two prototype 'above floor' engine diesel-electric multiple-units were constructed by BREL in 1981 and classified as 210. One 3-car and one 4-car unit were introduced, each having different technical and power equipment. Two powered Driving cars emerged — a DMBS and a DMS. The DMBS (illustrated) houses a Paxman 6RP200 power unit developing 840kW; this car has a small guard's compartment/luggage space and seating for 28 second class passengers, access being by passenger-operated double leaf sliding doors. The DMS (not illustrated) has an MTU 12V296 TC11 engine developing 850kW and provides accommodation for 45 second class passengers. The 4-car unit with its DMBS leading, departs from Acton on a Reading service in the summer of 1984.*
Colin J. Marsden

Above:
*Two types of intermediate Trailer were constructed, both being based on the same body design; one a TS and the other a TC with lavatory. The TS (illustrated) accommodates 84 passengers and access is by two pairs of double leaf doors. The area between the two sets of doors on the TC vehicle is for first class occupation. Trailers are mounted on BT13 bogies and underframe equipment consists mainly of air and brake modules.*
Colin J. Marsden

Below:
*Two DTS cars were built to operate at the non-powered end of both units. These cars seat 74 passengers and again have two pairs of double leaf doors on each side, the driver/guard having their own (sliding) door just to the rear of the cab position. The front end equipment consists of marker/tail and headlights, a centre Tightlock coupler and a drum box below containing all electrical/air connections. The 3-car set, No 210.002, is illustrated. Both sets are presently allocated to RG and usually operate on London/Reading/Oxford duties; livery is blue/grey.* Colin J. Marsden

# Class 253, 254 Trailer Vehicles

| | | | |
|---|---|---|---|
| **Car Type:** | TF | TS | TGS |
| **Car Numbers:** | 41003-41176 | 42003-42341 | 44000-44101 |
| **Former Numbers:** | — | — | — |
| **Introduced:** | 1976-82 | 1976-82 | 1976-82 |
| **Built by:** | BREL Derby | BREL Derby | BREL Derby |
| **Engine Manufacturer:** | — | — | — |
| **Horsepower (total):** | — | — | — |
| **Weight of Car:** | 33.6 tonnes | 33.6 tonnes | 33.4 tonnes |
| **Length over Body:** | 17.42m | 17.42m | 17.42m |
| **Height of Car:** | 3.81m | 3.81m | 3.81m |
| **Width of Car:** | 2.74m | 2.74m | 2.74m |
| **Brake Type:** | Air | Air | Air |
| **Maximum Speed:** | 125mph (201km/hr) | 125mph (201km/hr) | 125mph (201km/hr) |
| **Seating:** | 48 First | 72 Second‡ | 63 Second |
| **Regions of Allocation:** | Eastern, Scottish, Western | Eastern, Scottish, Western | Eastern, Scottish, Western |
| **Depots of Allocation:** | BN, EC, HT, LA, NL, OO, PM | BN, EC, HT, LA, NL, OO, PM | BN, EC, HT, LA, NL, OO, PM |
| **Works responsible for overhauls:** | Derby | Derby | Derby |

* All stored.
† Cars allocated to ER classified TRFB.
†† Excluding 40404-40413 (see TRB).
‡ Some cars seat 76 Second.

Above:
*The IC125 or High Speed Train sets have been included in this volume as their basic style is based on the DMU system. Class 253 sets are allocated to Old Oak Common, Bristol (St Philips Marsh) and Laira for internal WR use. Similar Class 253s are also used in a revised formation on the North East-South West, and Midland main line diagrams. WR internal sets are usually formed DM/TF/TF/TRUB or TRSB/TS/TS/TS/TGS/DM. Set No 253.024 passes Worth in the summer of 1982, with a Plymouth-Paddington service.*
Colin J. Marsden

| TRUB† | TRSB | TRFK | TFLK | TRB |
|---|---|---|---|---|
| 40700-40757 | 40401-40437†† | 40501-40511 | 40513 | 40204-40213 |
| 40300-40357 | 40001-40037 | — | — | 40004-40013 |
| 1976-82 | 1976-82 | 1976-82 | 1983 | 1976-82 |
| BREL Derby | BREL Derby | BREL Derby | BREL Derby | BREL Derby |
| — | — | — | — | — |
| — | — | — | — | — |
| 38.1 tonnes | 36.1 tonnes | 37.1 tonnes | 37.1 tonnes | 36.1 tonnes |
| 17.42m | 17.42m | 17.42. | 17.42m | 17.42m |
| 3.81m | 3.81m | 3.81m | 3.81m | 3.81m |
| 2.74m | 2.74m | 2.74m | 2.74m | 2.74m |
| Air | Air | Air | Air | Air |
| 125mph (201km/hr) | 125mph (201km/hr) | 125mph (201km/hr) | 125mph (201km/hr) | 125mph (201km/hr) |
| 17 Unclassified | 35 Second | 24 First | 16 First | 23 Second |
| Eastern, Scottish, Western | Western | Eastern | Eastern | Western |
| BN, EC, HT, LA, NL, PM | LA, OO, PM | NL | BN | LA, OO, PM |
| Derby | Derby | Derby | Derby | Derby |

Above:
*IC125s allocated to the ER/ScR are classified 254 but today a number of sets incorporate former Class 253 vehicles re-allocated from WR to ER. Class 254 sets are usually formed DM/TF/TF/TRUB/TS/TS/TS/TS/TGS/DM, however the first 11 sets have the TRUB and adjoining TS replaced by a TRUK and TRSB. Although this is the correct position, ER/ScR sets are prone to misformation, and it is not uncommon to find sets in service with additional TS cars, or indeed running with odd vehicles missing. An 8-car ER set is illustrated formed: TF/TF/TRUK/TRSB/TS/TS/TS/TGS.* Colin J. Marsden

Above left:
*Thirteen WR-allocated Class 253 sets are dedicated for North East-South West services being formed with an additional TS in place of one TF. This was introduced as there was a greater requirement on this route for second class accommodation. A North East-South West set led by power car No 43170 passes along the sea wall at Teignmouth with a Plymouth-Newcastle train.* Colin J. Marsden

Centre left and below:
*The external appearance of Trailer First (TF) and Trailer Second (TS) cars is identical except for the yellow band above the windows and the figure '1' on the doors of the first class vehicles. Underframe mounted equipment is all kept inside air smoothed boxes which are normally branded with letters of the alphabet to assist staff in locating equipment. Toilets are located at each end of each car. In the first plate TF No 41020 is illustrated, while the second plate shows TS No 42095. Although externally identical, the seating layout is quite different. On TS cars accommodation is for 72 (and in some cases 76) in the 2+2 mode, while in the TF cars there are only 48 seats in the 2+1 style.*
Both: Colin J. Marsden

Above:
*TGS coach detail, with guard's van and office nearest the camera. These TGS vehicles are formed one in each set with the guard's accommodation nearest the power car. The TGS car is basically a TS with guard's accommodation at one end. Passenger accommodation is provided for 63 persons with one toilet. TGS No 44016 stands at Reading in this view.* Colin J. Marsden

Below:
*Three different refreshment vehicles for IC125 sets have been built, the most numerous being the TRUB of which there are 58. In these vehicles there are 17 unclassified seats. The next largest class is the TRSB (illustrated) of which 37 were built. These accommodate 35 second class passengers. (Some of these vehicles have been rebuilt in early 1985 and now classified as TRB and accommodate 23 passengers.) The third and smallest fleet of refreshment cars are the TRUK type of which 20 were built, but only 11 now remain in use. The others have either been rebuilt or stored for possible future use. TRSB No 40036, now numbered 40436, is illustrated, clearly showing the between vehicle connections and the absence of side buffers.* Colin J. Marsden

Above:
*In 1983 TRUK No 40513 allocated to Bounds Green was converted into an executive lounge car with full cooking facilities with accommodation for 16 passengers and reclassified TFLK. The vehicle is available for private hire at special rates and operates within scheduled IC125 formations. The coach is painted in the latest InterCity livery and was photographed at King's Cross.* Colin J. Marsden

Below:
*There are two types of IC125 Driving Car in existence, those incorporating guard's facilities and classified DMB, and those built without the facility and classified DM. From the exterior the only recognition difference between the two types is an additional window towards the rear of the coach on DMBs. A DMB is illustrated from its inner end, showing the window, door and livery details.* Colin J. Marsden